ALAN WILKINS

ROMAN ARTILLERY

SHIRE ARCHAEOLOGY

2

Cover illustrations:
(Left) The one-talent *ballista*. Winding the slider forward. (Photograph by the author)
(Top right) Testing the *cheiroballistra*'s bolt velocity with a Chrony laser instrument.
(Photograph by the author)
(Bottom right) Vitruvius' *scorpio*, built by Tom Feeley from the author's research.
(Photograph by Tom Feeley)

British Library Cataloguing in Publication Data:
Wilkins, Alan
Roman artillery. – (Shire archaeology; 86)
1. Artillery – History
2. Rome – Army – Artillery
I. Title
355.8'2513'0937
ISBN 0 7478 0575 X

Published in 2003 by
SHIRE PUBLICATIONS LTD
Cromwell House, Church Street, Princes Risborough,
Buckinghamshire HP27 9AA, UK.
(Website: www.shirebooks.co.uk)

Series Editor: James Dyer.

Number 86 in the Shire Archaeology series.

ISBN 0 7478 0575 X.

First published 2003.

Printed in Great Britain by
CIT Printing Services, Press Buildings,
Merlins Bridge, Haverfordwest, Pembrokeshire SA61 1XF.

Contents

List of illustrations

Acknowledgements

The untimely death of Dr Eric Marsden in his late forties robbed Greek and Roman studies of a brilliant mind. I have tried to keep up the momentum of his research, attempting fresh reconstructions based firmly on the manuscript evidence and archaeological finds. All those working in this field owe an immense debt to Marsden and to a long line of scholars and enthusiasts, outstanding among whom were the text editor Carl Wescher and the experimental archaeologist Erwin Schramm.

Professor Dr Dietwulf Baatz has long maintained an eagle-eyed watch on the discoveries of catapult parts, publishing them with exemplary clarity. I am very grateful to him for advice and for allowing me to reproduce some of his drawings and photographs. It is a great delight to acknowledge the considerable help and constant encouragement of Mrs Margaret Marsden and of Dr John Marsden, Eric's son. I have benefited from correspondence or conversations with many people, notably Don Acklam, Lindsay Allason-Jones, the late John Anstee, Caroline Baillie, Duncan Campbell, Tom Feeley, Rex Harpham, Mark Hassall, Aitor Iriarte, Simon James, Carole Kirsopp, Gordon Macdonald, Christos Makrypoulias, Steve Ralphs, Pam Rose, David Sim, Digby Stevenson and Carol van Driel Murray. The credit for tackling the daunting challenge of building the one-talent *ballista* goes to BBC producers Helen Thomas, George Williams and the team of craftsmen and specialists. I am grateful to Adam Hart-Davis and producer Martin Mortimore for challenging me to reconstruct Dionysius' repeating bolt-shooter. My colleagues in the Roman Military Research Society and Paul and Christine Jones have helped with the field tests. Permission to use illustrations has been given by The Society of Antiquaries of London, Cambridge University Library of Air Photographs, Simon James, Len Morgan, Tom Feeley, the Ermine Street Guard, Dumfries Museum, Saalburg Museum and Staatliche Museum of Berlin. The Victoria and Albert Museum, London, kindly allowed photography of the casts of Trajan's Column. The staff of The British Museum were extremely helpful in allowing photography and weighing of the Qasr Ibrim stone shot.

It will be obvious that I owe a large and continuing debt to Len Morgan for realising my ideas so brilliantly. The superb quality of his reconstructions of the *scorpio* and *cheiroballistra* can be seen in the following pages and at the displays of the Roman Military Research Society. Sir Ian Richmond started my interest in the subject with the loan of a book on Schramm's reconstructions. My son Ian has maintained a fine computer set-up for me, and my wife Margery has shown endless patience in allowing me to give priority to the Roman world rather than to that of twenty-first-century house maintenance. This book is for her.

Glossary

Antonine: dating to the reigns of Antoninus Pius, Marcus Aurelius and Commodus, AD 138–92.

Ballista (**plural** *ballistae*): stone-throwing catapult (but by AD 100 used for a bolt-shooter).

Ballistarium: artillery emplacement (see figure 56).

Ballistarius (**plural** *ballistarii*): artilleryman, artillery mechanic.

Carroballista (**plural** *carroballistae*): bolt-shooter mounted on a cart (see figure 26).

Case and slider: the two components of the stock of a catapult (see figure 15).

Catapulta (**plural** *catapultae*): bolt-shooting catapult.

Cheiroballistra/*manuballista*: the revised design of bolt-shooter, introduced by AD 101–2.

Euthytone: 'stretched straight', describing a bolt-shooter whose springs are mounted in a frame with stanchions (upright beams) that from above appear to be in a straight line (see figure 23).

Hadrianic: dating to the reign of Hadrian, AD 117–38.

Hole-carriers: the horizontal beams forming the top and bottom of the spring-frame, and pierced with holes for the rope-springs and their washers.

Palintone: 'stretched back', describing a catapult whose springs are mounted in a frame with stanchions that are visibly staggered and not in a straight line, allowing the arms to travel in a greater arc than in a euthytone catapult (see figure 23).

Scorpio (**plural** *scorpiones*): a scorpion, either an alternative word for *catapulta* (q.v.) or a specific size of small bolt-shooter – the Larger or the Smaller Scorpion (page 16).

Spring-frame: the frame containing the rope 'springs' (see diagram opposite).

Stanchions, centre- and side-: the upright beams of the spring-frame.

Three-span: shooting a bolt three times a hand span – 27 Roman inches (68 cm) long. A popular size, combining portability with power.

Torsion catapult: so called because the springs of sinew-rope are stretched very tightly around the washer bars, and then torsion (twisting) is applied to them with a spanner, creating an enormous amount of stored energy in the rope 'spring'. The action of winding back the arms increases the torsion.

Two-cubit: shooting a bolt two cubits – 36 Roman inches (90 cm) long.

Universal joint: the flexible link between the stand and the stock of the catapult (see figure 18).

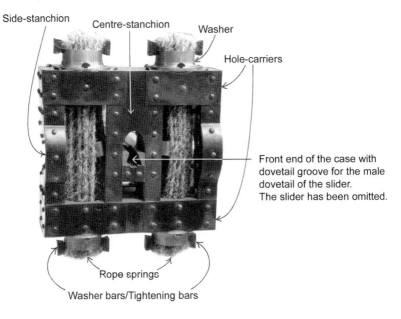

Reconstructed spring-frame of the Caminreal bolt-shooter, viewed from the front.

Weights and measures

1 Greek *mina* = 0.436 kg   1 *talent* = 26.196 kg   1 Roman *libra* (pound) = 0.327 kg
1 Greek *dactyl* = 19.268 mm   1 cubit = 46.2 cm   1 Roman *uncia* (inch) = 24.6 mm

Vitruvius' list of stone shot weights and corresponding spring-hole diameters

Weight of shot		Spring-hole diameter	
librae	kg	*unciae*	cm
2	0.655	5	12.3
4	1.31	6	14.76
6	1.96	7	17.22
10	3.27	8	19.68
20	6.55	10	24.6
40	13.1	12³/₄	31.3
60	19.65	14¹/₈	34.75
80	26.2	15	36.9
120	39.3	17¹/₂	43
160	52.4	20	49.2
180	58.95	21	51.6
200	65.5	22	54.1
240	78.6	23	56.5
360	117.9	24	59

(Based on Marsden)

1
Introduction

This is an introduction to the catapults of the Roman army, their dominance in the warfare of the western world for over a thousand years and their importance in the history of technology. There is a vast amount of material on this subject in the form of written sources, archaeological evidence and modern attempts at reconstruction. After examining the Greek origins of artillery, this account concentrates on the catapults used by Roman armies from the time of Caesar onwards.

Because only a small fraction of the written records of the Greek and Roman world has survived, the importance of the remaining artillery texts is greater than their face value as descriptions of machines of war. A few technical works on other subjects exist, but artillery is the one field of Greek and Roman applied technology for which there is extensive, detailed evidence. This is because of the survival of several technical manuals by specialist artillery engineers, in particular the Greeks Philon and Heron and the Roman Vitruvius (see chapter 14). As well as recording lists of parts and dimensions, they provide details of the development of catapult design, the workshop methods of engineers, their solutions to problems and their willingness to push forward into uncharted areas of mathematics, physics and metallurgy. There are also numerous passages describing artillery in action in the works of Greek and Roman historians, many of whom, such as Caesar, Arrian and Ammianus, were the officers who deployed these machines.

Greek artillery engineers are the first known users of cube root equations; they used devices such as straight and rotary ratchets, winches, multiple pulley systems, horizontal sliding dovetails, flexible universal joint bearings, screw threads and the enormous energy stored in stretched and twisted sinew rope-springs. The *Polybolos* or 'Multi-shooter', a repeating bolt-shooter designed by Dionysius of Alexandria c.300 BC, employs double-chain drive, a cam mechanism translating linear into rotary motion, and automatic systems for feeding the bolts and engaging and releasing the trigger. Similar devices were in everyday use for non-military purposes, but without the artillery manuals some of them would be unrecorded and others imperfectly understood. The Greek engineers' bold ideas for catapults powered by bronze springs or compressed air pistons outstripped the limitations of contemporary technology.

Their torsion-powered catapults were adopted and developed by the Roman army. They were the most powerful missile projectors of their time and had a considerable influence on events in the western world from Africa to Britain from their invention *c.*350 BC. They are still recorded as being in use by Byzantine armies in the eleventh century AD. No other weapon shooting heavy missiles has dominated the art of warfare for so long.

2
Greek origins

The object of catapult construction is to project the missile over a great
distance and strike a hard blow at a given target.
(Heron of Alexandria, *Belopoiika* 74)

The historian Diodorus states that artillery was invented in 399 BC by
Greek engineers working for the tyrant Dionysius I of Syracuse, during
a period of warfare between the Greek cities of Sicily and Italy and the
Carthaginians. Dionysius equipped his army with weapons whose
superior firepower devastated and demoralised his enemies.

The word catapult is Greek: *katapaltes* from the verb *katapallein*, 'to
hurl down'. It is used to describe a missile-projecting machine for
knocking down soldiers and structures, and which employs mechanical
means to produce a far superior performance to that achievable by
hand-operated weapons like the bow or the sling.

There is a limit to the pull that can be achieved by an archer's arm
and shoulder muscles. Most modern archery enthusiasts use a bow
with considerably less than a 45 kg pull. The skeletal remains of the
'massively boned' longbow archers on Henry VIII's flagship, the *Mary
Rose*, suggest that they were capable of exerting a pull of 45 to 78 kg.
Sir Ralph Payne-Gallwey estimates that a 68 to 72 kg pull was required
to draw the most powerful Turkish composite bows.

It was the ancestor of these Turkish bows that was in standard use by
most armies in Dionysius' day. The Greeks had gained their knowledge
of it from their Black Sea trading contacts with the Scythians, whose
skill as archers became famed and feared throughout the Greek world.
It was constructed of an inner layer of horn, a central core of wood and
an outer layer of sinew. The action of drawing the bow compressed the
horn and stretched the sinew. The combined properties of the three
materials made the bow so powerful that when unstrung it sprang back
to almost a reverse profile (figure 1).

The widespread use of this weapon throughout the Mediterranean
world made it very difficult for any one army to gain an advantage
over its opponents through missile power, except by producing
superior numbers of archers and longer lasting salvoes of arrows.
By offering high wages Dionysius attracted to Syracuse large
numbers of expert craftsmen. From the results that they achieved it
is reasonable to assume that he not only ordered them to produce
enormous quantities of standard weapons but also encouraged them
to experiment with new designs.

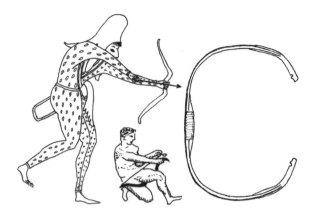

1. (From left to right) Scythian archer (from an Athenian vase painting). Stringing a composite bow (from a coin of Thebes). A Turkish bow unstrung (Doge's Palace arsenal, Venice).

The *gastraphetes*

The weapon that they invented was almost certainly the *gastraphetes* ('belly-bow'), a version of the composite bow enlarged to increase its range and strike-power beyond those of the hand-drawn weapon. Bows of spring steel do not appear until the fourteenth century AD.

Once Dionysius' engineers had made a bow that was too powerful to be drawn by hand, they devised an ingenious robotic replacement for the archer's arms, hands and fingers (figure 2). The left arm that extends

2. (Left) Spanning Schramm's reconstruction of a belly-bow. Note the operator's grip on the handles of the curved stomach-bar, and the help afforded by his overhanging stomach. (After Schramm 1918/1980)
(Right) Enlarged, winched composite bow from above. (After Marsden)

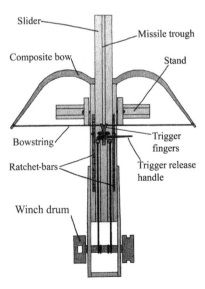

the bow was replaced by a long wooden stock consisting of a case and a slider. The grip of the left hand on the bow was effected by metal clamps that fastened the bow to the front of the case. The action of drawing the bow was achieved by a metal trigger, mimicking the archer's fingers, fitted to the rear of the wooden slider, on top of which was a shallow groove to guide the arrow. The slider moved in a dovetailed groove on top of the case. The archer drew the bow by resting the end of the slider on the ground and using his body-weight to push with his stomach against a curved component fastened to the rear of the case (figure 2). As the case was forced downwards, pawls on either side of the slider moved backwards along two toothed ratchet-bars on the case, locking into the ratchets as the weapon was spanned. An average person might achieve a 68 kg stomach pressure; someone heavier might expect to span a weapon of 84–91 kg.

The advantages of the belly-bow over the hand-bow would be either greater range with arrows of identical weight, or greater penetrative power with heavier arrows at similar or shorter ranges. It is easy to imagine the consternation and carnage among Dionysius' enemies, such as the unfortunate Carthaginians, who knew nothing of Dionysius' new weapon and believed that they were well out of range.

The introduction of the winch and stand

Bruised stomachs apart, there was clearly a limit to the power of the pull-back achieved by body-weight; and the curved stomach-bar was eventually replaced by a winch, enabling the artilleryman to exert almost unlimited pull-back on the bowstring, thus allowing bows of remarkable size to be produced, capable of hurling stones as well as heavy arrows (figure 2). The introduction of the winch also solved a problem that still affects present-day archers: the power of the bow being limited by the physical strength of its operator. The author's winch-powered reconstruction of the *cheiroballistra* (figure 39) is regularly operated by 'artillerymen' of all sizes and ages, from sixteen to seventy years, and its draw weight is 335 kg. Winches were operated by straight capstan bars, as is clearly shown on the Cupid Gem (figure 30). The crank-handle was either not known or rarely used by Greek and Roman engineers. Heavy-duty stands were devised to support the catapults at a convenient height for loading and aiming.

The *gastraphetes* designed by Zopyrus of Tarentum (Taranto in Italy) was mounted on a stand and had a bow 2.77 metres long. It shot simultaneously two bolts 1.85 metres in length and 1.9 dactyls (3.6 cm) in diameter, indicating that the engineers were under instructions to increase the volume of missiles as well as their range and weight. It had taken them less than forty years to develop a weapon capable of outshooting the legendary Scythian bow, and, even more impressive, one capable of hurling heavy stones and so outshooting the sling. With the invention of the winched *gastraphetes* the art of war had entered a new phase. Curiously, the term *gastraphetes* was retained for these catapults even though they were not loaded by stomach pressure.

There is no evidence for the ranges achieved by Dionysius' catapults, but the startling impression they made on those who witnessed their power is evidenced by Plutarch's story of the Spartan king Agesilaus. On seeing a piece of artillery for the first time the king exclaimed, 'By Heracles! A man's courage in battle is no use any more'. The occasion was probably 368/367 BC, when Dionysius sent troops to help the Spartans defeat the Arcadians and Argives in a victory described by Xenophon as 'tearless'. 'Tearless' suggests a relatively bloodless victory achieved because the new catapults enabled the Spartans and Syracusans to shoot up the enemy while staying out of range.

However, a remarkable discovery was about to be made; one that would unleash far greater projectile power and would ultimately make it possible to construct a small catapult, the Roman *cheiroballistra/ manuballista*, which was not much larger than the Scythian hand-bow but whose maximum range with a heavy bolt was probably over 300 metres.

The invention of torsion-powered artillery

> Seeking to make the arms of the bow more powerful, but being unable to achieve their objective by means of the horned [composite] bows, they made the arms of stronger wood and larger than the arms of a bow; they assembled a frame of four stout beams … wound sinew-rope round the horizontal beams … pushed one of the arms through the middle of the sinew-ropes.
>
> (Heron, *Belopoiika* 81)

This is the beginning of Heron's description of an early version of a torsion catapult, a completely novel design, which replaced the *gastraphetes'* composite bow. Two separate wooden arms were inserted into two vertical skeins or springs of sinew-rope mounted in a stout frame of hardwood reinforced with iron plates. Each strand of the rope was pre-stretched by winches around top and bottom iron washer-bars. The iron washer-bars were slotted into revolving bronze cylinders that allowed the skeins to be twisted, forcing the bow arms forward. This twisting or torsion of the rope-springs was further increased when the arms were drawn back by winch, storing a massive amount of energy in the sinew (figure 3).

Torsion catapults are one of those developments in the history of

3. Operator's view of Dr Eric Marsden's torsion catapult, shooting three-span (68 cm) bolts. The frame is a replica of the earlier Greek design, using two separate upright stanchions in the centre. The later Roman version replaced these with a single substantial centre-stanchion, as in figure 20. (Photograph: Eric Marsden)

technology that seem to appear from nowhere, like the ball- and roller-bearings on the Roman ships in Lake Nemi. Circumstantial evidence seems to point to engineers in the pay of Philip II of Macedon, the father of Alexander the Great, as inventing the principle of torsion sometime before 340 BC. Alexander put catapults to good use in sieges such as that of Tyre and in driving off Persian and Scythian opposition at river crossings.

Rapid improvements were made to the design by the engineers of Alexandria and Rhodes, so that by 300 BC catapults could project lethal bolts from two hand spans (45 cm) and three spans (68 cm) in length up to a hefty man-size spear four cubits (1.84 metres) long, and stones could be shot that weighed up to a staggering 3 talents (78.6 kg). Doubts have been expressed as to whether stones as heavy as 78.6 kg could have been shot from torsion catapults, but stone balls of this calibre have been found at Hellenistic sites such as Pergamon (Turkey) and Rhodes. Demetrius Poliorcetes in 307 BC fitted the three-talent size into the lower floors of his 41 metre high siege tower at Salamis on Cyprus. Philon of Byzantium lists eight sizes of stone ammunition from 10 *minae* (4.3 kg) to 3 talents (78.6 kg). Vitruvius, Augustus' catapult engineer, has a more detailed list (see Glossary), which starts at 2 *librae* (0.65 kg), and goes one size beyond 240 *librae* (3 talents) to a 360 *librae* (118 kg) stone. Vitruvius' special oval washers and larger spring-frame enabled more spring-cord to be inserted (see page 64), so that the stone-throwers of his day were more powerful size for size than Philon's. The largest shot in regular use by the Roman army seems to be the one-talent (26.2 kg), found on sites from Israel to Britain. A one-talent machine has been recreated by the BBC (see page 57).

All but the heaviest of these bolt or stone missiles could be projected to ranges far greater than war arrows shot from hand-bows, or pebbles or lead bullets propelled from slings, and their impact could kill or cripple personnel even at the end of their travel.

By *c*.275 BC catapult design had become so thoroughly refined that Alexandrian engineers were able to devise a set of formulae for calculating the ideal size of every component, based on the length of the bolt or the weight of the stone shot.

3
The menace of the new weapon

If the superiority of the non-torsion catapults over conventional bows had been remarkable, the leap in range and power achieved by torsion machines was sensational. There was a rush by non-Greek countries to acquire them, corresponding to the modern arms race to acquire atomic weapons.

Roman armies encountered them in the early third century BC through contact with the Greek cities of southern Italy and Sicily. To gain a decisive advantage over the maritime power of Carthage in the First Punic War (264 to 241 BC) they were compelled to acquire two unfamiliar weapons, warships and artillery, and the skills to use them, both with the help of Greek engineers. There is one piece of important evidence for the numbers of catapults available to one army. Livy records that during the Second Punic War (218 to 201 BC) Scipio captured the main Carthaginian base in Spain at New Carthage, modern Cartagena. He discovered the following artillery in Hannibal's arsenal:

120 *catapultae* of the largest kind
281 *catapultae* of the smaller kind
23 larger *ballistae*
52 smaller *ballistae*
A vast number of larger and smaller *scorpiones*, armour and weapons.
(Livy, *History of Rome* XXVI, 47, 5–6)

Catapultae are bolt-shooters, *scorpiones* are the smallest sizes of bolt-shooters and *ballistae* are stone-throwers. Without counting the scorpions, bolt-shooters outnumbered stone-throwers by more than five to one. A similar ratio is found in the work of the late Roman writer Vegetius, who says that there were fifty-five catapults and ten *onagri* (one-arm stone-throwers) in each legion. The reason for the disparity is that stone-throwers were constructed to project far heavier missiles and were therefore heavier, more complicated and expensive machines, requiring more spring-rope and probably larger teams of operators. Only the smaller calibres of stone-thrower were light enough to be manoeuvred on the battlefield.

The 120 catapults of the largest kind probably shot bolts three or four cubits long, the 281 of the smaller kind two-cubit bolts. It is almost certain that the larger scorpions were three-spans, shooting bolts three hand spans long (68 cm), and that the smaller scorpions were two-span/one-cubit catapults whose bolts were 45 cm long.

4. Large, well-finished stone shot from the Archaeological Park, Carthage (Tunisia). From their sizes (note the sandal) they are estimated as weighing 1½ talents (39 kg, the two left-hand ones), 1 talent (26 kg, the right-hand pair) and ½ talent (13 kg, the centre stone). They may date from the destruction of Carthage by the Romans in 146 BC; see page 15. (Photograph: the author)

In 149 BC, Carthage surrendered its artillery to the Romans, totalling 'up to two thousand bolt-shooting and stone-throwing catapults' (Appian, *Lybike* 80), another indication of the very large numbers of catapults involved in the warfare of that time.

4
Caesar's artillery

In late August of 55 BC, warriors lining the white cliffs of Britain's southern shore watched the approach of Caesar's large invasion fleet, carrying a force of two legions. The warriors' command of the shore persuaded Caesar to move seven miles to the east to find a more favourable spot for a landing on 'an open and level beach'. Caesar makes excuses for his troops' reluctance to jump down in armour into the heavy channel swell to face the Britons who were boldly hurling their missiles from the beach and from horseback as they rode into the water. His solution was to order his warships to row quickly out of the mass of transport vessels to a position on the exposed flank of the enemy and drive them away 'with slings, arrows and catapults'. This manoeuvre 'was of great help to our men', says Caesar, 'for the natives were terrified by the shape of the ships, the motion of the oars and the unfamiliar kind of artillery; they halted and retreated, but only a short distance' (*Gallic War* IV, 25).

The artillery (Caesar uses the word *tormenta*, 'torsion machines') would probably have been projecting stones of about grapefruit size, and 68 and 90 cm bolts from three-span and two-cubit scorpions, hitting the Britons at ranges well beyond the accompanying showers of slingshot and arrows. The catapults would have gained additional range because they were mounted high up on the warships' towers.

So catapults were most often used by Roman armies in combination with slingshot and arrows to create a dense, long-range hailstorm causing injury or death over a wide area. The sling bullets striking the Britons on the beach, if they were of the leaden type, were probably capable of killing at ranges of up to at least 80 metres, and causing serious injuries at twice that range. Modern slingers on Ibiza can hit a 1 metre square target at 200 metres.

A Roman composite bow shooting an arrow of about 85 grams may have had a maximum range of 250 metres and an effective killing range of up to 200 metres. Eastern enemies of Rome continued to use the Scythian type of composite bow with great effect, most notably the Parthians, whose unceasing showers of arrows destroyed the army of Caesar's colleague Crassus at Carrhae in Mesopotamia, modern Iraq, two years after the landing in Britain.

Three years after the British invasion Caesar again used tower-mounted artillery at Alesia, Mont Auxois in central France, in his confrontation with the coalition of Gallic tribes led by Vercingetorix. Caesar relied on artillery and rapidly constructed earthworks to compensate for the fact

5. Reconstruction of Caesar's siege lines at Alesia (52 BC) in the Archéodrome archaeological park at Beaune (Burgundy, France). The photograph shows the wide 'killing zone' of obstacles in front of the palisaded rampart and two ditches, including sharp stakes set in the honeycomb of pits nicknamed 'lilies', similar to the pits outside the forts at Rough Castle on the Antonine Wall, Scotland, and at Wallsend on Hadrian's Wall. Caesar mentions the large numbers of missiles discharged by his artillery, and describes Gauls shot from the rampart or impaled on the stakes. (Photograph: the author)

that he was heavily outnumbered by the 80,000 Gauls under Vercingetorix whom he had surrounded in their hillfort, and the 258,000 Gauls who had arrived to rescue them. He constructed eleven Roman miles of inward-facing and fifteen miles of outward-facing palisaded ramparts with towers every 24 metres, and created a broad 'killing zone' of traps and obstacles where artillery stones and bolts, arrows, spears and slingshot could pick off the Gauls (figure 5). The 1991–6 excavations have added to the tally of weapons first found on the site by Napoleon III's excavations. Two stone catapult balls found near Camp A weigh 4.6 and 7.5 kg and come from medium-size stone-throwers of 14 and 23 *librae*. Considerable numbers of Roman twin-barbed arrowheads have been excavated. A group of twenty-four lead sling bullets includes two that are inscribed with the name of Titus Labienus, one of Caesar's generals, perhaps the commander of that sector of the battle.

5
The bolt-shooter: accuracy and effects

Dramatic archaeological evidence comes from the Claudian invasion of Britain in AD 43, when the future emperor Vespasian, commanding the Second Legion, fought thirty battles, defeated two tribes and captured more than twenty hillforts and the Isle of Wight. Archaeologists believe that they have located evidence of his artillery in action at two hillforts in Dorset.

At Maiden Castle near Dorchester Sir Mortimer Wheeler interpreted his discovery of forty skeletons of Britons buried in shallow graves close to the east gate as a 'war cemetery' and evidence of a great massacre of the British defenders, with the legionaries storming the gate under the cover of artillery fire. However, re-examination of the fifty-two skeletons now discovered reveals that only fourteen have battle wounds. There is one artillery victim with the iron point of a bolt in his spine (figure 6). Wheeler's battle casualty figures have been disproved, but the technique of assault under cover of artillery fire is authentic and a Vespasian speciality. An eyewitness describes him clearing enemy battlements with such a barrage from his three legions at the siege of

6. Iron bolt-head from a catapult lodged in the spine of a Briton buried at Maiden Castle, Dorset. The bolt has travelled uphill and entered around his belly button. (Skeleton now in the Dorset County Museum, Dorchester. Photograph © The Society of Antiquaries of London)

Jotapata (Palestine) in AD 69:

> Vespasian ordered his artillery, numbering a total of 150 machines …
> to fire at the defenders on the wall. In a coordinated barrage the catapults
> sent bolts whistling through the air, the stone-throwers shot stones
> weighing one talent, fire was launched and a mass of arrows. This made
> it impossible for the Jews to man the wall or even the area behind it that
> was strafed by the missiles. For a mass of Arabian archers, spearmen
> and slingers were in action along with the artillery.
>
> (Josephus, *History of the Jewish War* III, 166–8)

Like most of the enemies of Rome, the Briton killed by the catapult bolt
would not have been wearing metal body armour. A writing tablet from
Vindolanda critical of British fighting tactics describes the 'wretched
Britons' (*Brittunculi*) as wearing no armour (*nudi*). Tests with a
reconstructed bolt-shooter of this period against steel plate (figure 40)
show that even if he had been wearing body armour he would have been
put out of action.

25 km to the north-east of Maiden Castle at the hillfort of Hod Hill,
unique proof of the accuracy of the bolt-shooter was found when Sir Ian
Richmond examined two large round huts that had come under attack.
A total of seventeen iron bolt-heads were found, most of them still
embedded in the chalk where they had landed, their wooden shafts
having rotted away. Sir Ian conjectured that they had been fired in an
arc starting with four bolts in the rectangular enclosure outside Hut 36a,
and one inside that hut. No fewer than eleven had landed inside Hut 37,
and only one had overshot to land in the adjacent Hut 43. The slope of
the site in the direction from which the bolts came, and the existence of
other huts on that alignment interfering with the line of sight, would
have made it necessary to shoot from a high viewpoint, such as the
rampart itself or a temporary tower (as in figure 52) overlooking the
rampart. The range from such a position would have been about 150–70
metres. Analysis of the shooting (figure 7) shows accuracy of the kind
that will regularly knock out troops and horses at this range.

Sir Ian suggested that the artillery attack was that of Vespasian's
Second Legion in AD 43 and that the chieftain's hut was selected as a
target to intimidate the defenders into surrendering. 'The lack of evidence
for an assault on the hillfort … would strongly suggest that capitulation
was then and there induced by showing dramatically what concentrated
fire could do.'

It is unlikely that this dramatic and attractive scenario will ever be
proved or disproved. An alternative possibility is that these bolts were
shot at a later date during target practice by the legionaries living in the

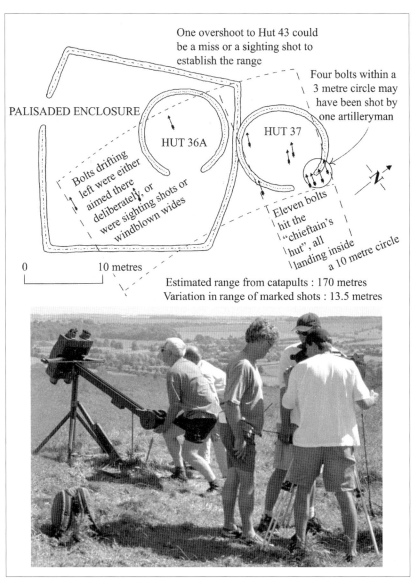

One overshoot to Hut 43 could
be a miss or a sighting shot to
establish the range

Four bolts within a
3 metre circle may
have been shot by
one artilleryman

PALISADED ENCLOSURE

HUT 37

HUT 36A

Bolts drifting
left were either
aimed there
deliberately, or
were sighting shots or
windblown wides

Eleven bolts
hit the
"chieftain's
hut", all
landing inside
a 10 metre circle

0   10 metres

Estimated range from catapults : 170 metres
Variation in range of marked shots : 13.5 metres

7. (Top) Unique evidence for the accuracy of Roman bolt-shooters. The author's analysis of
Sir Ian Richmond's Hod Hill 'target'. (After Richmond)
(Bottom) Filming for Adam Hart-Davis's programme *What the Romans Did for Us*. Len
Morgan is aiming the three-span *scorpio* at the BBC target on the site of Hut 37, 150 metres
away. Forty-eight of the fifty bolts shot during filming landed within a 10 metre circle, the
diameter of Hut 37. This is an authentic technique of aiming the *scorpio* by sighting over the
top of the spring-frame. (Photograph: Margery Wilkins)

Roman fort that was built in the corner of the hillfort. In May 2000 the BBC filmed Len Morgan and the author shooting at the position of Hut 37 with the Vitruvian three-span *scorpio* then used by the legions (figure 7).

Writers of all periods confirm the accuracy of the bolt-shooters, which were more suited to precision shooting than were stone-throwers. Caesar records that at the siege of the Gallic hillfort of Avaricum (52 BC) a *scorpio* killed a Gaul attempting to set fire to the Roman siegeworks and then killed a succession of Gauls who picked up the same firebrand. During the siege of Leptis Magna in the Civil War in Africa (46 BC) a decurion commanding a cavalry squadron was struck and pinned to his horse by accurate fire from a *scorpio*. The incident not only caused the rest of his squadron to flee back in terror to their camp but also made them scared of attacking the town again. The fact that these are Roman cavalrymen on the receiving end of a Roman missile familiar to them makes this a particularly impressive example of the panic caused by artillery fire. Livy describes the more controlled reaction of the Roman general Scipio in 205 BC when attacking the walls of Locri:

> Scipio had advanced towards the wall when the man who happened to be standing next to him was struck by a scorpion. The danger implied by this incident alarmed him and he moved his camp well out of the range of missiles.
>
> (Livy, *History of Rome* XXIX, 7, 6)

6
Reconstructing the bolt-shooter

It is possible to reconstruct the bolt-shooting catapult of late Republican and early Imperial armies with a high degree of accuracy because of the detailed description by Augustus' artillery engineer Vitruvius, the illustrations on relief carvings, and major finds of iron and bronze catapult parts.

By the early twentieth century many of the problems in interpreting the difficult artillery texts had been solved by French and German pioneers. Napoleon III encouraged Generals Dufour and de Reffye to make the first serious attempts to reconstruct Greek and Roman catapults. Another imperialist, Kaiser Wilhelm II, backed Erwin Schramm's impressive reconstructions at the beginning of the twentieth century (figure 8).

In 1969 and 1971 Dr Eric Marsden published his masterly study *Greek and Roman Artillery*, setting the subject in its historical framework and providing an excellent edition of the most important Greek texts. Since 1971 many artillery parts have been identified and catalogued by Professor Dr Dietwulf Baatz, but Marsden's early death prevented him from incorporating them in new reconstructions of the machines. The

8. Erwin Schramm (centre) demonstrating his reconstruction of Vitruvius' *ballista* to Kaiser Wilhelm II at the Saalburg fort on 16th June 1904. The Kaiser was almost a twentieth-century victim of the *ballista* when the bowstring slipped under the missile and lifted it vertically (see 'Bowstring problems' on page 58). (Photograph: Saalburg Museum)

9. Schramm's fine reconstruction at the Saalburg Museum of a bolt-shooter's iron plating, bronze washers and iron washer-bars discovered at Ampurias in Spain in 1912. The plating of the centre-stanchion is missing, but it survives on the second iron frame plating found at Caminreal (Teruel, Spain) in 1983 (figure 10). The spring diameter is 74 mm, exactly the size of a three-span. It is unusual in that the front of the outer stanchions is straight and not curved to compensate for the weakness caused by the semicircular cut-out for the arms, as recommended by the artillery texts and found on the Caminreal frame. (Photograph: the author)

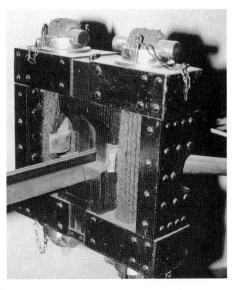

author has taken up this research, and the reconstructions in this book are based firmly on a fresh examination of the manuscripts of the artillery writers and the archaeological evidence. Field testing of these reconstructions has enabled limited assessment to be made of the weapons' characteristics.

Evidence for the design of the Roman torsion bolt-shooter

The main written evidence is that of Vitruvius' detailed list of parts and measurements in his *De architectura*; but his diagrams have not survived, and his text has suffered damage and losses. The problems of deciphering his text are discussed on page 55.

The only archaeological find known in Schramm's day was the iron plating and bronze washers from a three-span *scorpio* frame found in 1912 at Ampurias (Spain) (figure 9). In 1983 the iron plating and bronze washers from a *scorpio* frame were found at Caminreal (Teruel), Spain (figure 10). Amongst the numerous finds of artillery washers are several from the

10. The reconstruction in Aalen Museum, Germany, of a bolt-shooter's iron plating, bronze washers and iron washer-bars discovered at Caminreal (Teruel, Spain) in 1983. The spring diameter of 8.4 cm makes it a machine of $3^{1}/_{3}$ span. See figure 17 for the author's suggested purpose of the lower hole in the centre-stanchion, left unused in this reconstruction. (Photograph: Len Morgan)

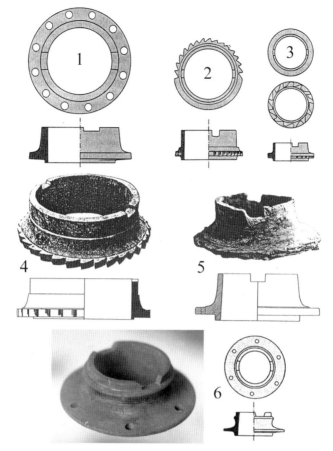

11. Washers presumed to be from bolt-shooters, from various sites and periods. Numbers 1, 2 and 3 are from the shipwreck at Mahdia (Tunisia) dated to the second quarter of the first century BC. Inner diameters (= spring diameters) are 85, 65 and 41 mm. Like number 4, numbers 2 and 3 use ratchet tracks to lock the washers into position, instead of the usual system of pins and holes. (4) Sunion (Greece); third century BC; inner diameter 130 mm. (5) Azaila (Spain); dated to the Sertorian Rebellion of 80–72 BC; inner diameter 94 mm. (6) Bath (England); inner diameter 34 mm. This small bronze washer might be from a training model; it had been deposited in the sacred spring, possibly by an artillery engineer as an offering to Sulis-Minerva. Dating from the second half of the first century or the first half of the second century AD.

shipwreck at Mahdia in Tunisia of the second quarter of the first century BC (figure 11). Finds from a military grave or pit of AD 69 outside the walls of Cremona, Italy, include a partially complete, inscribed three-span *scorpio*'s battle-shield (figure 12), with washers.

Constructing the spring-frame

The tensioning and twisting of the two rope-springs applied enormous forces of compression and torsion to the frame in which they were set. Before the invention of artillery Greek engineers had used hardwood

TI CLAVDIO DRVSI F CAESARE AVGVSTO
GERMANICO

12. The battle-shield from a three-span bolt-shooter of the Fourth Macedonian Legion, found with its washers in a military grave outside the walls of Cremona (Italy) along with human bones and two or three damaged skulls. These probably belonged to victims of the battle of AD 69 between the forces of Vitellius and Vespasian, recorded by Tacitus in *Histories* III, 29. The consular names date its manufacture to AD 45. The probable position of slider and bolt has been added in black. Because the bolt is always positioned half-way up the spring-frame, it is clear that the shield has lost a section at the top. The author has restored the shield's original outline and Claudius' imperial titles. The rectangular hole at the base matches the lower hole on the Caminreal frame (figure 10) and is interpreted by the author as allowing a wedge to be driven in from the front to lock the spring-frame to the case (see figures 17 and 20). (Photograph: Dietwulf Baatz)

frames reinforced with metal plates for cranes and other large machinery. These were the materials used for catapult frames until the introduction of the Roman army's all-metal spring-frame at the end of the first century AD. The constructional techniques required were within the skills of any competent carpenter, blacksmith or bronze worker, and well within those of the specialist engineers in a Roman legion's workshop. Catapults were constructed, repaired and operated by the legions, although some auxiliary regiments may have been allowed to operate them from the late second or early third century AD. An important papyrus from Egypt records two days' production in a legionary workshop making catapult frames and a variety of arms and armour with a supplementary unskilled workforce of auxiliary soldiers, camp servants and civilians. Casting round bronze components and finishing them on lathes was a long-established procedure; lathe marks can be seen on several catapult washers, for example on the Bath washer in figure 11. Perhaps the most difficult operation was forging iron plates in the large sizes required to clad the spring-frames.

The formula established by the Greek engineers was that all the components are measured in fractions or multiplications of the spring-hole diameter, which is one-ninth of the length of the bolt. For the standard three-span *scorpio* the spring-hole will be 3 Roman inches (74 mm) in diameter. The Latin word for 'spring-hole', *foramen*, is translated as 'h.'.

In order to channel the enormous compressive force of the rope-spring away from the hole-carriers and down the stanchions, the distance from the spring-hole to the stanchions was kept to a minimum. Vitruvius gives this distance as ^{1}/4 h.

Vitruvius' square 6 h. by 6 h. frame may have been the textbook standard. He says that the frame can be made higher (*anatonus*, 'oversprung') or lower (*catatonus*, 'undersprung'). The Ampurias, Caminreal and Cremona finds are all from spring-frames, ^{3}/4 h., ^{7}/8 h. and ^{1}/3 h. undersprung respectively. Undersprung frames may have been the norm and may have produced increased range and therefore the ability to hit an approaching enemy sooner.

The plating covering the spring-frame

> Let the four outside angles on the sides and faces be bound with iron plates and bronze bolts or nails.
>
> (Vitruvius, *De architectura* X, 10, 3)

Even before the discovery of the Ampurias plating in 1912, the existence of plating was confirmed by the Vedennius relief (figure 13). It has been suggested that plating was only there to protect the wood

13. The detailed relief of a *scorpio* on the left side of the tombstone of artillery engineer C. Vedennius Moderatus, dated to *c*.AD 100, now in the Chiaramonti Gallery of the Vatican Museum. Vedennius was appointed by Vespasian and Domitian as an engineer (*arcitectus*) at the Imperial Arsenal in Rome. Heavy plating is riveted on to the front of the hole-carriers. Note the incised circles on the side of the side-stanchion, representing the rivet-heads found on the Ampurias and Caminreal frames (figures 9 and 10). Also depicted are the washers, the ends of the washer-bars, the rope-springs, the four hollow-eyed pins locking the washers, the bowstring passing round the arms, and what appears to be the point of a bolt or the end of the slider in the aperture of the battle-shield. (Photograph: the author)

14. Stylised representation of the front of a bolt-shooting catapult on the Altar of Zeus from Pergamon (Turkey). This is the earliest evidence for the use of curved arms, which allow a few extra degrees of forward arm travel and thus increase the energy stored in the rope-springs (see figure 23). Dated to the reign of Eumenes II, 197–160/159 BC. (Photograph: Staatliche Museen, Berlin)

against fire attack (see page 44). However, Heron (*Belopoiika* 92–3), describing the stone-thrower's stanchions, says that plates must be nailed to both sides of a stanchion, and plates encasing its double tenons must be fixed with nails 'so that the side-stanchion, bound securely on all sides, may be able to withstand the strain'. Plating the tenons, which are sunk out of sight in the mortise slots of the hole-carriers (figure 42), can have nothing to do with fireproofing.

The arms

The length of the arm is 7 h., its thickness at the bottom is $^5/8$ h., at the top $^7/16$ h. Its curvature is 8 h.

(Vitruvius, *De architectura* X, 10, 5)

Confirmation for the arm curvature comes from the relief on the Pergamon altar (figure 14). Curved arms allowed the bowstring to end up closer to the spring-frame (figures 16 and 23) and the arms to travel in a greater arc, thus storing a greater amount of energy.

The case (i.e. the stock) and the slider

Vitruvius describes a laminated construction for the case, with a central beam and two side- or cheek-pieces, all 19 h. long (figure 15).

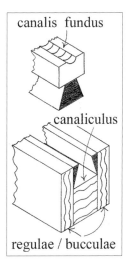

15. Isometric cross-sections of the *canalis fundus* ('base of the channel'), that is the slider (top), and the case, which is laminated from a central *canaliculus* ('channel') and two *regulae/bucculae* ('side-pieces'). The case is 19 h. long and 1 h. wide and high. The three pieces forming the sliding dovetail are marked in black and can be cut from one piece of timber.

16. (Right) This is the artilleryman's view of the *scorpio*'s winch box, drums, ratchets, handspike, and trigger mechanism, with a three-span bolt loaded into the channel of the slider. The advantage of the curved arms, allowing a few extra degrees of forward arm travel, is proved by the proximity of the bowstring to the spring-frame. Note the spanner for turning the washers, on the ground to the left of the winch. (Photograph: the author)

17. (Below) The wedge system for locking the case to the spring-frame; this is the author's explanation for the rectangular holes in the Cremona battle-shield (figure 12) and the Caminreal frame (figure 10). The upper wedge is permanently fixed to the underside of the case. The lower wedge is driven in from the front of the spring-frame. The wedges are visible in figures 19 and 20. (Photograph: the author)

The length of the slider is 16 h., its thickness <$^6/16$> h., its width $^1/2$h..
(*ibid.* X, 10, 4)

The Cremona battle-shield (figure 12) supports a reading of $^6/16$ h. for the thickness of the slider, a good example of an archaeological find providing a measurement where the figure in the manuscripts of Vitruvius is missing or corrupt.

The trigger assembly (figure 16)
The general form of these components was worked out by Schramm and was probably similar for bolt-shooters of all periods.

The winch box (figure 16)
The manuscript figure for its height should be amended from 'S' to 'IS' (see page 55). Then it does resemble three sides of a box.

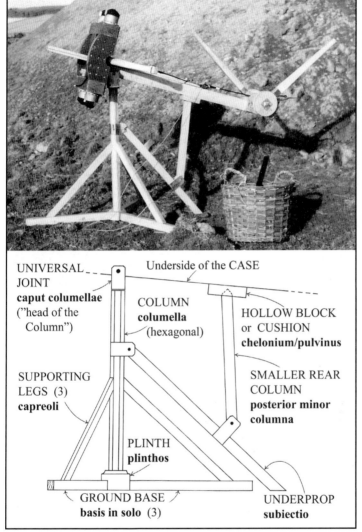

UNIVERSAL JOINT
caput columellae ("head of the Column")

Underside of the CASE

COLUMN **columella** (hexagonal)

HOLLOW BLOCK or CUSHION **chelonium/pulvinus**

SUPPORTING LEGS (3) **capreoli**

SMALLER REAR COLUMN **posterior minor columna**

PLINTH **plinthos**

GROUND BASE **basis in solo** (3)

UNDERPROP **subiectio**

The stand and universal joint (figure 18)

The extraordinarily detailed list of parts for the stand contrasts sharply with the lack of detail for more vital components. Vitruvius' text has lost some information. Where, for example, are the washers?

The *caput columellae*, 'head of the column', is ingeniously translated by Marsden as 'universal joint'. This key component allows the case to swivel in all directions and gives the artilleryman total freedom to adjust the aim. Robert Hooke (1635–1703) is usually credited with

19. The enemy's view of the Vitruvian *scorpio* built by Tom Feeley, incorporating a battle-shield based on the layout of the 1887 Cremona find (figure 12). The Cremona shield is described as 'a flat iron plate covered with a thin plating of copper'. This would make it strong enough to provide protection for the rope-springs from enemy fire-arrows and other missiles, and partial protection from the weather. It also adds to the impressive look of the machine. (Photograph: Tom Feeley)

inventing this type of joint, but it was almost certainly used on Greek cranes even before its application to artillery.

The standard bolts

The central hole in the Cremona battle-shield (figure 12) provides evidence for the bolt's width and flights. The shaft must have had a diameter no greater than 18 mm on a three-span *scorpio*, with flights limited to a width of 8 mm. There is no evidence for the length of the flights or whether they were made of feathers or leather. The Greek word *pteron* means 'feather' or 'wing', but also anything that is wing-like. Long flights made of leather (figure 20) are preferred by modern re-enactors who reuse their bolts.

No complete bolt for the Vitruvian type of catapult has been

20. General view of the three-span *scorpio* built by Len Morgan from the author's interpretation. The bolts are of 18 mm dowelling and have leather flights and bodkin points. Their average weight is 200 grams. This is the type of bolt-shooter used by Greek, Roman and other armies from the third century BC onwards. Its deadly accuracy is vouched for by Caesar (page 23), who also used it to clear the beach of Britons in 55 BC (page 18). It was probably a machine of this type that shot a tight group of bolts at the 'chieftain's hut' at Hod Hill, Dorset, in an impressive display of marksmanship (figure 7). The battle-shield has been omitted in order to show the rope-springs and centre-stanchion. Also visible is the removable wedge that locks the spring-frame to the case, protruding from the lower hole in the centre-stanchion (see figure 17). (Photograph: the author)

found. Hundreds of iron missile heads survive in museums all over the Roman Empire; almost all of them are too corroded to make estimates of their original weights feasible. Furthermore, except for the foreshafts from Qasr Ibrim, discussed below, the wooden shafts and flights have rotted away. Because of this it is difficult to be sure which missile heads belong to arrows, or catapult bolts, or even javelins. However, one type of missile head (figure 22) is generally agreed to be from a catapult bolt – the larger tapering, pyramidal bodkin point mounted on a hollow socket. This identification is confirmed by its use on the later Dura Europos type of catapult bolts, whose wooden shafts have survived (page 54 and figure 41) and whose uncorroded heads can be weighed.

The Qasr Ibrim foreshafts and iron bodkin heads

A special design of bolt-head plus shaft has been identified, contemporary with Vitruvius himself. For a few years from 23 BC Roman legionaries occupied the fortified stronghold of Qasr Ibrim, poised on high cliffs above the Nile near Abu Simbel. The finds sealed in the layers of this exciting multi-period site are in amazing condition. They include large numbers of stone shot, many inscribed (figure 49), and several iron bodkin points with tangs, mounted on specially turned and shaped hardwood foreshafts. Similar iron heads and incomplete hardwood foreshafts found at Haltern and Vindonissa in Germany have fostered arguments over whether they were short but complete missiles,

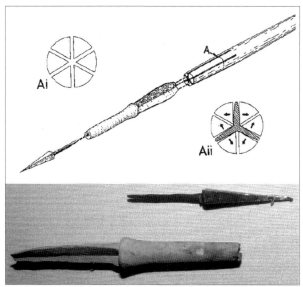

21. (Top) Reconstruction of the assembly of a tanged bolt-head and hardwood foreshaft on to a softwood mainshaft. The mainshaft receives three saw-cuts, creating grooves into which the three vanes of the foreshaft can be pushed, similar to the modern method of attaching the cruciform plastic flights to darts. (After James and Taylor) (Bottom) Foreshaft and bolt-head from Qasr Ibrim. Lathe marks are visible on the shaft. (The British Museum. Photograph: the author)

perhaps intended for use with crossbows, or whether they were foreshafts whose triple 'vanes' were spliced on to long mainshafts with flights and shot from catapults. The author agrees with the latter interpretation (figure 21) based on the Qasr Ibrim examples. The mainshaft may have been of softwood, and the hardwood foreshaft would have guaranteed extended penetration of the iron point before the shaft snapped. Similar iron points with tapering tangs are now being reported at many sites, such as Alesia and Vindolanda. Some authorities have doubted whether artillerymen bothered to recover their missiles, but the time estimated by Dr David Sim and the author for the construction of a single Vitruvian bolt-head plus shaft is about one hour, making each bolt too valuable to discard, certainly during target practice.

The rope-springs and the bolt-shooter's performance

The power of the catapult depended entirely on the quality of the rope-springs. According to the artillery writers, sinew-rope was much preferred.

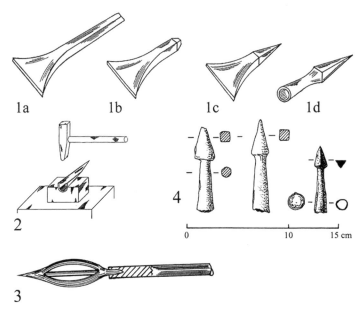

22. Dr David Sim's reconstruction of the methods of manufacturing artillery bolt-heads. (1a–d) Stages in making a standard bodkin point. (2) Creating the socket. (3) A fire arrowhead (after Sim). (4) Catapult bolt-heads from Caesar's siege lines at Alesia. The larger left-hand pair have square bodkin points and are of a size suited to a two-cubit machine shooting bolts 90 cm long. The other has a triangular point and was possibly shot from a three-span *scorpio*. Bodkin points were also standard for medieval crossbows and longbows (after Brouquier-Reddé).

The only clear information on the performance of a bolt-shooter includes the weight of sinew used. A contemporary of Vitruvius, Athenaeus Mechanicus, describes the ranges recorded by the engineer Agesistratos: 'he so outstripped his predecessors that anyone reporting the facts on his behalf is not easily believed. For his three-span catapult shot three and a half stades with twelve *minae* of sinew' (647 metres, with 5.24 kg of sinew-rope). Athenaeus implies that to shoot a three-span bolt, probably weighing about 200 grams, 647 metres was an exceptional achievement, one that beat previous recorded ranges and was somewhat difficult to believe. Agesistratos was a specialist artillery engineer who probably tuned his catapult to perfection and chose the time and weather. The performance of an average legionary catapult in battle conditions can only be guessed at. Schramm's three-span reconstruction of the Ampurias catapult armed with horsehair achieved 305 metres in 1918 and was still capable of 285 metres sixty-four years later. If it had been equipped with curved arms (figure 23), allowing greater arm travel and giving the springs more twist, it would have shot even further. This gives credibility to the modern estimate of 400 metres as a minimum range easily achievable by legionary bolt-shooters with springs of sinew.

The key references are extracted below.

> You must use sinews, either from the shoulder or back, and from all animals except pigs ... it has been found that the more exercised sinews of an animal happen to have more *eutonia* ['elasticity', or perhaps 'efficiency when stretched'], for example the sinews from the feet of deer, from the neck of a bull ... The spring-cord on the arms is also made of women's hair, because being fine, long and fed with plenty of oil it acquires much *eutonia* when plaited, with the result that it does not fall short of the power obtained from sinews.
>
> (Heron, *Belopoiika* 110–12)

23. Diagrams to show the limits imposed on the arc of arm travel by the euthytone frame of the Vitruvian bolt-shooter (left) and the palintone frame of the Vitruvian *ballista* (right). For the meanings of euthytone and palintone see the glossary and pages 40-2.

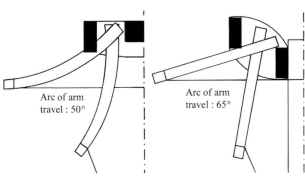

Arc of arm travel : 50°

Arc of arm travel : 65°

> ... onagers, ballistas and other catapults are of no use unless strung
> with sinew ropes. However horsehair from tails and manes is claimed to
> be usable for ballistas. There is no doubt that women's hair is just as
> excellent in catapults, as Roman crises have proved.
>
> (Vegetius, *Epitoma rei militaris* IV, 9)

As to the use of women's hair, the number of occasions when women
were shorn in the cause of their city's defence has probably been
exaggerated. During the siege of Carthage in 147–6 BC Strabo records
that 'slave-girls provided hair for the catapults'. There is no doubt that a
spring made of a skein of sinew-rope gave a markedly superior
performance to one of horsehair. The properties of individual or small
groups of sinew fibres have been analysed by Dr John Landels, who
concluded that the catapult engineers had chosen 'what was probably
the best material available to them, since its energy-storing capacity is,
believe it or not, higher per unit weight than spring steel'. Dr Caroline
Baillie and master bowyer Steve Ralphs tested short lengths of a variety
of ropes for the BBC *ballista* programme. They confirmed that sinew-
rope gives back an exceptionally high percentage of the energy stored
in it. They also found that horsehair rope was poor in this respect, a fact
that confirms the author's experience with it. Schramm and others tried
without success to make rope from sinew. In 1996 such rope was
successfully manufactured by Digby Stevenson, using the backstrap
sinew that runs from the loin to the backbone of cattle.

The labour-intensive process involves drying the sinew, then pounding
it with a mallet to break it into fibres and splitting these until they are
fine enough to be spun into yarn. Heron refers to a machine for plaiting
ropes but gives no details. Heron also mentions the Achilles tendon of
deer, and Steve Ralphs made rope from Achilles tendons for the BBC
test. Vindolanda Tablet II, 343 is a letter, possibly dating from AD 122,
from an Octavius who appears to be either a civilian contractor or a
centurion responsible for supplying the army with hides, grain and
other materials. The first item on his list is 100 Roman pounds of sinew
(32.75 kg), possibly intended for catapult springs. This would fit in
with the known presence at that date of legionaries at Vindolanda,
perhaps in preparation for the building of Hadrian's Wall. The
manufacture of sinew-rope may well have been put out to civilian
contract.

Fitting, tensioning and twisting the rope-springs

The Greek engineers had discovered that the energy-storing properties
of sinew-rope could be markedly improved by pre-stretching it, and a
special stretching frame with winches is described by Vitruvius and

Heron. The skeins of spring-cord were wound around top and bottom iron washer-bars, which were slotted into revolving bronze cylinders conventionally translated as 'washers' (figures 20 and 38). Each strand is stretched, says Heron, until it loses one-third of its diameter. Vitruvius says that the first tensioned strand is plucked to sound a musical note and that all subsequent strands are tuned to the same note. Heron describes how to get extra strands through the washers by driving blunt iron bars into the skein with a mallet to open up more space. The rope-springs' capacity to store energy could be further increased by applying a large spanner and twisting the washer-bars and washers towards the front of the catapult. This twisting or torsion of the rope-springs was further increased when the arms were winched back. The description 'torsion catapult' derives from this.

7
The new design: the metal-frame *cheiroballistra*

There have always been hopes of finding 'lost' manuscripts of Greek and Latin authors. Napoleon III's Bibliothèque Impériale employed a manuscript hunter, Minoïde Minas. On his death a manuscript that included the artillery texts was found amongst his papers, with a note that it had been discovered in 1843 in the monastery on Mount Athos. The information from it was incorporated into a magnificent edition of the Greek artillery writers by the Alsace scholar Carl Wescher, published 'by order of the Emperor' in 1867.

Wescher's analysis showed that the Minas manuscript contained the

24. Two of the five illustrations of catapults on Trajan's Column in Rome (Scene LXVI, Casts 164–6), from the scenes depicting Trajan's first campaign against the Dacians in AD 101–2. Two machines with the characteristic arched strut of the *Cheiroballistra* text are sited on the rampart of a Roman fort (top left). In the foreground a machine manned by two legionaries is mounted on a raised platform of logs, apparently part of outworks strengthening the fort. It has been suggested that the sculptor has used an exploded diagram, and that the platform had a log roof and sides giving full protective cover to the crew. On the evidence of Trajan's Column, a two-man crew was standard, as on the light and medium machine guns of modern armies. (Cast in the Victoria and Albert Museum, London. Photograph: the author)

earliest and best copy of the writers. He used it to produce an improved version of the highly intriguing Greek document entitled 'Heron's Construction and Dimensions of the *Cheiroballistra*' (*cheiroballistra = manuballista*, 'hand catapult'), one of the most important technical manuscripts to have survived from classical times. This describes eight mechanical parts, each illustrated with a coloured diagram and beginning with the Greek letter kappa ('K'). German artillery specialists had already declared the work to be indecipherable. In 1877 the French civil engineer Victor Prou published his interpretation of it as a description of a bolt-shooting catapult powered by bronze springs, of the type described by Philon. Unfortunately his imagination fed on the title and led him to invent cast bronze human hands to hold the spring-frames. In 1906 the German classicist Professor Rudolf Schneider dismissed Prou's reconstruction as a work of fantasy and declared that the text was a short extract from a technical lexicon listing unconnected parts alphabetically. He conceded that some parts might be from catapults, but believed the title *Cheiroballistra* to have been erroneously added by a Byzantine scribe. There was a staggering ninety-four years following Prou's reconstruction during which the *Cheiroballistra* text was discredited or ignored.

In 1971 Dr Eric Marsden reinstated the document, identifying it as a description of a bolt-shooting catapult of a new design, equipped with metal instead of wooden spring-frames, and with an arched strut identical to that on the catapults shown on Trajan's Column in Rome (figure 24). Thus Marsden established the machine as a bolt-shooter issued to the

25. Detail of the rampart catapult in figure 24. Note the object on the right behind the legionary's helmet, discussed on page 45. The sculptors of the Column are so inconsistent in their versions of these catapults that they cannot have been familiar with them. Sir Ian Richmond's suggestion that they were working from sketches made on campaign may well be valid in this case. (Cast in the Museo della Civiltà Romana, EUR, Rome. Photograph: the author)

Roman army from the time of Trajan onwards. His interpretation was vindicated when in 1974 Nicolae Gudea and Dietwulf Baatz published several iron catapult parts found in the late Roman forts on the Danube at Gornea and Orșova (Romania). They identified them from the manuscript illustrations as a large version of the *cheiroballistra*'s arched strut and several sizes of the metal spring-frames (figures 32 and 34).

Tragically, Eric Marsden died before he could suggest a fresh interpretation of the machine based on this new evidence. In 1994 the author published a reconstruction based on a revised Greek text and translation and the Romanian finds. From this Len Morgan, the distinguished reconstructor of Roman artefacts, built the fully operational machine seen in these pages. There is complete agreement amongst scholars that the *Cheiroballistra* text is indeed a description of a bolt-shooting catapult powered by torsion springs, the washers and washer-bars for the rope-springs being clearly described and illustrated. However, there are several signs that the text is incomplete. Because it does not include a description of a winch or stand some scholars do not believe that the catapult was a standard winched torsion machine. They have attempted to prove that it was a much less powerful one operated either as a belly-bow or, to downgrade it even further, as one spanned by hand and firing small darts weighing less than a third of the weight of the standard war arrow. It would have been pointless to equip the army with a catapult with a feeble performance inferior to that of hand-bows. 'The object of catapult construction', Heron and Philon remind us, 'is to project the missile over a great distance and strike a hard blow at a given target.'

There are two irrefutable reasons for believing the torsion *cheiroballistra* to be a standard winched catapult. Firstly, Heron states categorically (*Belopoiika* 84–5) that torsion catapults developed so much power that the belly-bow's stomach-bar had to be replaced with a winch, with a pulley system added for the larger machines. On the author's reconstruction the draw pull has been measured at 335 kg, nearly five times that required to draw the most powerful hand-bow or belly-bow. Secondly, one critical measurement, the cross-section of the *cheiroballistra*'s wooden case, has been increased by more than 25 per cent over that of the comparable size of the Vitruvian *scorpio*, implying that the *cheiroballistra* was more, not less, powerful than the traditional design of winched catapult.

The *cheiroballistra*'s all-metal spring-frame

This revised design of bolt-shooter had increased power because it allowed the arms to move through a greater arc. This was achieved firstly by borrowing the palintone style of frame used on stone-throwing

26. Trajan's Column, Scene XL. Two *carroballistae* (cart-mounted *ballistae*) in action, shooting over the heads of advancing troops. Vegetius says that each legion had fifty-five of these. Each cart is pulled by two mules. The rear legionary on the nearer machine is operating a winch handle, the drum being visible under his hand. The size of a Roman cart, as estimated from the standard wheel spacing of 5 Roman feet, suggests that there was room for a larger version of the arched strut catapult than that in the *Cheiroballistra* text, perhaps with a rope-spring diameter of 74 mm (3 Roman inches), as on the Lyon catapult (figure 33). The far catapult is shown loaded with two bolts, which may be factually accurate (Zopyrus' *gastraphetes*, page 12, and the Hatra catapults, page 69, could shoot two missiles at once), or a mistake by the sculptor, or his way of suggesting a storm of missiles. (Photograph: the author)

27. Trajan's Column, Scene LXVI. A legionary soldier accompanying either a *carroballista* or a standard cart transporting a *ballista*, perhaps to an emplacement as in figure 24. The catapults on the Column are mounted on a base with a stout support column braced by two 45 degree struts. (Photograph: the author)

28. Trajan's Column, Scene LXVI, Cast 169. Two Dacians on a stockade with a Roman catapult. This must have been captured either during Trajan's campaign of AD 101–2, or some fifteen years earlier when the Dacians had killed general Cornelius Fuscus and seized the catapults and engineers of *Legio V Alaudae*, whose return was negotiated by Trajan during his campaign. If indeed these two Dacians are in possession of one of Fuscus' machines, then the introduction of these arched strut catapults can be put forward to AD 86–7. (Cast in the Museo della Civiltà Romana, EUR, Rome. Photograph: the author)

ballistae. The Vitruvian bolt-shooter had an all-in-one euthytone frame with the stanchions in a straight line, limiting the forward travel of the arms when they hit the stanchions. To produce the greater power needed to project stones, two separate spring-frames were used, with their stanchions out of line in palintone configuration, allowing increased arm travel. The borrowing of a *ballista*'s palintone frame probably explains why the term *ballista* was transferred to the new bolt-shooting *manuballistae* and *carroballistae*. The idea of modifying a palintone stone-thrower to shoot a bolt was not new. In 49 BC the citizens of Marseille used very large ones to shoot enormous spike-tipped beams 12 Roman feet (3.56 metres) long at Caesar's siege lines; he says that they passed right through four thicknesses of wickerwork screens before sticking in the ground. Agesistratos used a palintone stone-thrower to hurl a four-cubit (1.84 metre) bolt four stades (740 metres).

Secondly, figure 29 shows that in comparison with the Vitruvian design the *cheiroballistra*'s spring-frames were pushed three times further apart. Some scholars believe that this was to allow the introduction of inward swinging arms, a nineteenth-century theory for which there is no ancient evidence. In fact increasing the distance between the slider and the rope-spring allowed vital extra degrees of rearward travel by the arms before arm and bowstring approached the undesirable in-line position, undesirable because it consumes initial spring energy before starting the forward movement of the bolt. The maximum angle between bowstring and arm at full pull-back should not exceed 150 degrees (as in figures 23 and 55). The arc traversed by the *cheiroballistra*'s arms is about 70 degrees, some 20 degrees greater than that of the Vitruvian

29. (Top) Artilleryman's view of the Vitruvian *scorpio*, with the all-in-one spring-frame preventing direct aiming along the missile and slider. The target must be viewed over the top of the frame, leaving uncertainty as to the correct elevation of the case.

(Bottom) The same view of the *cheiroballistra/manuballista*. The two spring-frames are spaced well apart, allowing increased arm arc, a stockier bolt (figure 41) and an unimpeded aim along the missile and slider, with further 'framing' of the target by means of the semicircular arch in the upper strut. (Photographs: the author)

ones. If inward-swinging arms had ever existed they would require the spring-frames to be mounted about half-way along the case. The Cupid Gem (figure 30) appears to be based on a bolt-shooter of the *cheiroballistra* type and shows the spring-frames mounted right at the front of the case.

The old wooden frames blocked off a clear line of sight to the enemy, and it was necessary to aim over the top of the frame or along the side. Now that there was no centre-stanchion, a totally unrestricted view of the enemy was opened up, and it was possible to aim along the shaft of the bolt, resulting in greater accuracy. The open framework allowed the approaching enemy to be followed at all times, however much he swerved, and in close combat the final shot could safely be delayed until a hit was certain and the bolt penetrated with maximum force. The open frame also allowed the missile to be followed throughout its trajectory and corrections to be easily judged. Experience supports Marsden's suggestion that accurate aiming could have been assisted by

30. (Top) The Cupid Gem. A plaster cast of a carved gem from a finger ring, the only known side-view of a Roman catapult. The gem cutter has created a witty version of Cupid firing an arrow, by arming the god with a weapon of enormously greater amorous firepower. Cupid is grasping a winch handle in each hand, the advantage of this double-ratchet system being speed of rewinding, with a continuous hold kept on both handles, and a push-pull action of the arms keeping the winch axle turning almost continuously. This results in an increased rate of fire, of vital importance to the artilleryman faced with hundreds of horsemen charging towards him. Other clearly cut details include the bowstring, winch rope, trigger, winch pawl, universal joint, and pinned joints on the stand. This type of stand is not the Vitruvian three-leg type and seems to be the same as those on Trajan's Column; therefore the gem probably shows a bolt-shooter of the arched-strut type. Was the double-ratchet system introduced with the arched-strut machines? (Photograph: Dietwulf Baatz)

(Bottom) The author's reconstruction of the *cheiroballistra*, with a two-handle winch system based on the Cupid Gem. The stand is based on the evidence of the Gem and Trajan's Column. Straight side-ratchets were chosen instead of the circular ratchets of Vitruvius' *scorpio* partly because this is a safer system if the winch rope breaks, and partly to be able to test and refute the theory that this machine was a belly-bow (page 40). (Photograph: the author)

relating the target to the arch in the upper strut.

The aperture for the bolt in the old centre-stanchion had to be small (figure 10) to avoid weakening the stanchion. The omission of this stanchion removed the restriction on the width of the bolts; a stockier, stronger bolt was designed, with more durable flights, a more stable flight path and greater wounding power (page 54). It also allowed the possibility of two bolts being shot at once (see page 69 and figure 26), and eliminated the risk of a bolt striking the centre-stanchion.

There are several incidents during the wars of the early Empire which prove that a wooden catapult was easily damaged or set on fire by enemy action, as in the siege of Jerusalem (Josephus, *Jewish War* V, 279–80, 286–7). The *cheiroballistra*'s metal framework made it fireproof. The catapults on Trajan's Column appear to have covers on their spring-frames (figure 27), a detail not found in the text, making it almost impossible to damage the rope-springs with fire or axe. The old-style battle-shields (figure 19) covered only the front of the springs. The Trajanic covers afforded all-round protection and would have been almost weatherproof, apart from the slit left for the traverse of the arms. Fire arrows had been shot from wooden-framed catapults since Hellenistic times. Fire-bolts (*malleoli*) and fire-spears (*falaricae*) are described by Vegetius as being launched from larger *ballistae* against wooden siege-towers (*Epitoma rei militaris* IV, 18) and ships (*ibid.* V, 44). They could be more safely used on this new design because of the fireproof framework and covers.

Ease of dismantling and repair was another advantage of the new design. If a Vitruvian wooden spring-frame developed a split or was damaged in battle, it could not be repaired on the spot, and it would be a workshop job to file off the rivet-heads and prise off the metal cladding. In contrast, the *cheiroballistra*'s metal spring-frame was built up from a number of bronze or iron components that were individually neither heavy nor bulky. Each was apparently linked to the next by removable pins or wedges, or by the interlocking of tenons with mortises. No rivets were needed. It would therefore have been possible to repair a machine with a damaged spring-cord on the battlefield, because each individual field-frame could be replaced by a spare ready fitted out with its pre-tensioned spring-cord, washers, arm and so on.

The *Cheiroballistra* text is unique among the artillery documents because it is the only one to give exact sizes for components in dactyls, rather than a system of proportions based on the size of the spring-hole. This may have been because it was the archetype, from which larger versions, such as the *carroballista* or the Lyon example (figure 33), were developed. There are four main manuscripts of the text: M (the Minas manuscript) and P in the Bibliothèque Nationale in Paris; V in

31. The *cheiroballistra*. Realisation of the trigger mechanism based on the text instructions and diagram. The claw-shaped trigger imitates the archer's two fingers on the bowstring. The 'snake' is the release lever that locks the claw over the bowstring. This is one of the nicknames given to the parts, probably by the *ballistarii* who operated the catapults. It does have a snake-like appearance, and when pulled back to release the claw it delivers the deadly sting. The tapering rear end of a Dura Europos type of bolt (figure 41) fits into the claw. (Photograph: the author)

the Vatican Library and F in the National Library in Vienna.

The following is necessarily a brief commentary on the eight parts.

kanones duo (two boards), i.e. case and slider

The Vitruvian wooden case and slider were retained; they were not the sort of components that could be translated into metal.

There is one new non-Vitruvian component, the crescent-shaped fitting attached to the end of the case. Those who have tried to downgrade this catapult to a belly-bow believe that this fitting was mounted horizontally as the equivalent of Heron's stomach-bar. However, the crescent-shaped fitting lacks the end handles of the stomach-bar seen in use in figure 2. On Trajan's Column, Scene LXVI (figure 25) there is something looking very like the rear end of the case, with the winch axle and a vertical crescent-shaped fitting.

kleisis (trigger mechanism) (figure 31)

This and Heron's diagram of the *gastraphetes* are the best evidence for artillery trigger design; no actual trigger parts have been identified.

kambestria (field-frames) (figure 32)

This is the simplest of solutions for a metal replacement of the Vitruvian spring-frame: two rings to hold the washers, spaced apart by two bars, one of which has the semicircular arm recess. The Greek name is the equivalent of the Latin *campestria*, frames for use in the field (*campus*), a reminder that these catapults were primarily intended for use on the battlefield rather than for static defence. The word *pittarion* used to describe the brackets attached to the bars is not found in any dictionary, and only when the Gornea and Orşova frames were identified was it realised that it simply means a bracket shaped like the Greek letter pi

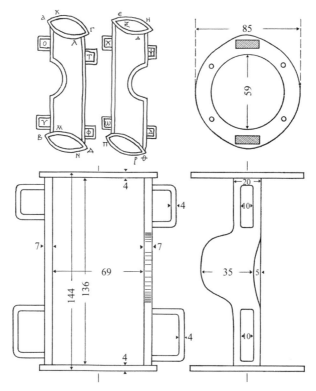

32. The *cheiroballistra*. Field-frames. (Top left) Codex M's drawing of the pair of frames. (Top right and below) The No. 2 iron frame discovered in the tower of the fort at Gornea on the Danube, dated to the late fourth century AD. This is only two-thirds the height of the *cheiroballistra* frames; its rings are slightly narrower and their internal diameter of 59 mm suggests that its missing washers would have allowed a rope-spring diameter of 2½ dactyls (48–9 mm). Note the pi-brackets attached to the bars (see page 45), and the semicircular recesses for the arms, similar to those on the Vitruvian wood frames (after Gudea and Baatz). The manuscripts' reading of a mere 1⅓ dactyls (24.3 mm) for the internal diameter of the washers and the diameter of the *cheiroballistra*'s rope-springs would make the catapult 'little more than a toy' (Marsden). The majority of scholars support a corrected reading of 2⅓ or 2½ dactyls (45 or 48 mm) for the rope-spring diameter (page 47), similar to that calculated for this Gornea No. 2 frame.

(π). For the suggested use for such brackets see figure 38.

kulindroi chalkoi (**bronze cylinders**) and *kanonia* (**bars**)

There does not seem to be any major difference between these and the earlier standard design of washers.

The manuscript reading for their internal diameter, the spring diameter, is a puny 1⅓ dactyls (24.3 mm). Marsden astutely pointed out that the two iron stanchions corresponding to the Vitruvian wooden side- and centre-stanchions are 3½ dactyls apart, and that Vitruvius (*De architectura* X, 10, 2) records that the distance from both stanchions to

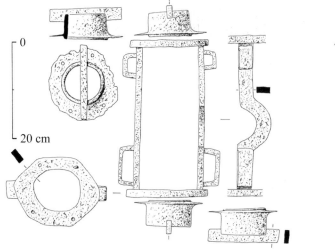

33. The *cheiroballistra*. The large iron field-frame complete with iron washers and bars found at Lyon (France). Its spring diameter of 75 mm (3 Roman inches) is the same as that of the old Vitruvian three-span *scorpio*, but its height is less. The spring volume is 1.86 litres compared with the Vitruvian 2.3 litres, but the increased arc of the arms may have made up all, or nearly all, of the difference. The Lyon catapult would have been of a size suitable for mounting on a cart as a *carroballista*. Two other large field-frames have been found, one at the late-fourth-century AD fort at Orşova on the Danube (estimated spring diameter 69–70 mm), and a bronze version in Morocco (estimated spring diameter 80 mm). (After Baatz and Feugère)

the spring-hole should be only $^1/_4$ h. On this basis the manuscript reading for the internal washer/spring diameter should be corrected to $2^1/_3$ dactyls. Figure 32 shows that this critical $^1/_4$ h. distance was indeed maintained on the Gornea metal field-frame, vindicating Marsden's correction.

kamarion (arch)

This component is named after the semicircular arch that is easily recognised in the manuscript diagram (figure 34). The Orşova arch is a 2.75 times enlargement of the *cheiroballistra*'s and presumably belonged to a large tower-mounted static version of the machine, appropriate for the defensive tactics of the late fourth century. The broken Orşova tenons display one intriguing detail, rectangular holes, which are not mentioned in the text. The author interprets them as holes to receive lugs to lock the arch in position. Similar holes are assumed to have been present on the tenons of the ladder (figure 37).

klimakion (ladder)

So far no ladder has been found. It has been reconstructed from the text measurements along with the limited help afforded by the diagram (figure 35). Whereas the arch is a comparatively slender top brace between the two field-frames, the ladder is an extremely strong

34. The *cheiroballistra*. The arch.
(a) Codex M's version. The forked
tenon ends have been turned through
90 degrees, there being no tradition
at that time of using two drawings
to show views from two different
planes. (b) Drawings of the huge
iron arch found in the late-fourth-
century fort at Orşova on the Danube
(after Gudea and Baatz). Note the
negligible difference between this
and the manuscript version, proving
that not all the manuscript drawings
have been corrupted by copying.
The Orşova arch is a 2.75 times
enlargement of the *cheiroballistra*'s
and must belong to a very large
tower-mounted machine, a Mons
Meg of its day. (c) Drawing of the
broken forked end of the Orşova
arch showing the rectangular holes
on one tenon. The author's
reconstruction of the catapult is
based on the assumption that these
are lug holes for locking the parts
together. The stippled drawings are
of the reconstructed forked end and
a side view of the arch, with
measurements in millimetres.

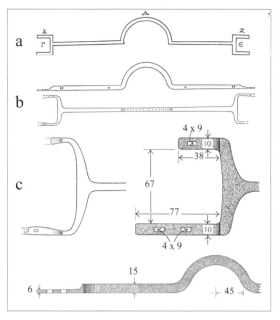

35. The *cheiroballistra*.
(Top) Codex P's drawing of the arch
and ladder. The side-poles and
tenons of the ladder are coloured red
in the manuscript, black in this
tracing. Centuries of copying have
resulted in several errors; for
example, the small T-clamps that
lock the case to the ladder have
become distorted and joined to the
ladder.
(Bottom) Codex M and Codex V's
drawings of the two-part arm.
Unfortunately all four copies of the
text end in mid sentence when they
are about to give the length of the
metal bars. Codex V's version seems
to show a dovetail groove in the
cones for the insertion of the bars.
The bars have been reconstructed in
steel tempered with the resilience
that Philon describes in the case of
'Celtic and Spanish swords'
(*Belopoiika* 71).

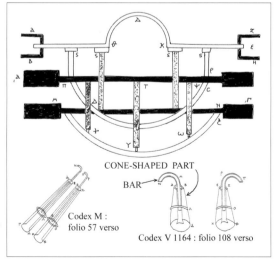

CONE-SHAPED PART

BAR

Codex M :
folio 57 verso

Codex V 1164 : folio 108 verso

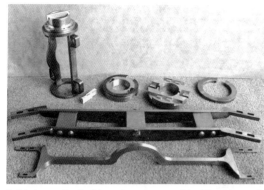

36. The *cheiroballistra*. The author's version of the parts of the front framework. (Front) The arch. Compare with figure 34. (Centre) The ladder. The rear side-pole is longer and is interpreted as setting up the 18 degree forward twist of the end tenons, which give the spring-frames their palintone character-istic. (Rear) From left to right: field-frame with the top bronze washer and bar; a pair of wedges to fit inside the pi-brackets and hold down the locking rings; a set of locking rings clamped together by a C-ring; the underside of a set of locking rings; a C-ring. The wedges and locking rings are the author's suggestion for missing parts (see figures 37 and 38). (Photograph: the author)

component that takes the weight of the field-frames, spring-cord, washers and arms, locks them rigidly in position and resists the enormous force of winding back and the shock of release.

The two beams forming the side rungs of the ladder are of different lengths. The reconstruction (figures 36 and 38) allows the longer beam to turn the end tenons at an angle of 18 degrees to the beams, setting up the palintone position of the field-frame bars and allowing the arms vital extra degrees of travel, measured at 70 degrees.

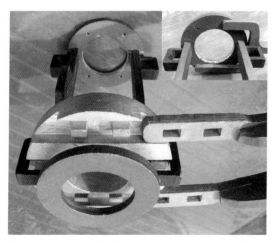

37. All but two reconstructions of the *cheiroballistra* join the arch to the field-frames by passing its tenons through the field-frames' pi-brackets. However, the shorter arch tenon (measurements in figure 34) is too short to do so. Other measurements lead to the conclusion that there are missing parts and that both arch and ladder were clamped to the inside surfaces of the field-frames' rings. (Inset photograph) The author's wooden model of the arch positioned under the field-frame's top ring; the lug holes have been omitted. (Main photograph) The model, showing the ladder's tenons ready to be gripped between the proposed locking rings and the rings of the field-frames. The bronze locking rings provide the mortise grooves for the tenons of the arch and ladder, and rectangular lugs in these grooves fit into the rectangular holes in the tenons, a system based on the evidence of the holes in the Orșova arch tenons (figure 34c). (Photographs: the author)

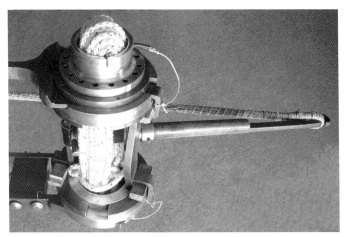

38. The left-hand section of the reconstruction of the *cheiroballistra*'s frame, from the front. The inner ends of the tenons of the arch and the ladder can be seen entering the mortise grooves in the bronze locking rings. Pairs of wooden wedges in the pi-brackets clamp down on iron C-rings, holding the two halves of each locking ring together. (Photograph: the author)

konoeide duo (two cone-shaped parts), i.e. arms

One of the apparent aims of this new design was to replace as many wooden parts as possible with metal ones. However, an arm consisting solely of a slim bar of metal would not have had the bulk to be gripped satisfactorily by the spring-cord. So these bars are joined to thick tapering cones, which provide the necessary bulk. Unfortunately our copies of the text stop in mid-sentence, just as they are about to mention the length of the metal bars and possibly the total length of each arm. The author's study of Vitruvius' stone-thrower (chapter 9) concludes that it had the same arm length as the bolt-shooter – seven times the spring-hole diameter. To discover a possible arm length for the *cheiroballistra*, a pair of 'telescopic' arms and bowstring were gradually lengthened until they allowed the slider to be fully retracted and the arms to lie almost parallel with the case (figure 39). The arms were found to be 17^1/2 dactyls long. If this figure is correct, it confirms that the spring-hole diameter should be 2^1/2 dactyls and that the standard arm length of 7 h. was retained.

Missing parts

Figure 37 explains why there must be parts not mentioned in the manuscripts, linking both arch and ladder to the field-frames.

8
Artillery in action: Arrian's battle plan

A single detailed Roman battle plan survives to show how artillery was deployed. In AD 134 Flavius Arrianus, the governor of Cappadocia (eastern Turkey), faced a large invading army of mounted spearmen, the Scythian Alani, highly respected as skilled riders and warriors. Arrian met them with his Fifteenth and Twelfth Legions and several auxiliary regiments of cavalry, horse-mounted archers, infantry and spearmen. He positioned the legions in the centre, with the higher ground on either wing held by auxiliary infantry with cavalry protection. 'The catapults are to take up positions on both wings, so that they can open fire on the enemy at extreme range' (Arrian, *Ektaxis* 19). The height will have increased the range of the catapults; some of the bolt-shooters may have been the easily manoeuvred *cheiroballistrai/manuballistae*. 'The catapults are also to be stationed behind the whole line of battle' (*ibid.*). To be able to fire over the single line of foot archers in front of them, the eight ranks of the legions and a screen of cavalry, most of

these must have been the larger, more powerful machines and would surely have included the cart-mounted *carroballistae* seen on Trajan's Column (figure 26), of which there were fifty-five in each legion according to Vegetius. There were probably many of the old wooden-frame bolt-shooters still in service – it would be wrong to suppose that they were withdrawn when the metal-frame catapults were introduced. Most of the stone-throwers would be of small to medium calibre, shooting orange to grapefruit sizes of shot, and of the traditional wooden frame design described in the next chapter.

39. The *cheiroballistra*. The catapult is ready to shoot a replica of the Dura Europos bolt (figure 41). The draw weight required to pull the bowstring fully back has been measured by Len Morgan as 335 kg, one-third of a tonne. This is nearly five times the pull exerted by the strongest archers, quoted on page 10. (Photograph: the author.)

There must be silence until the enemy come within missile range. Just as they do so, the whole army is to shout in unison the loudest and most blood-curdling battle-cry to Enualios [Mars], the catapults are to fire both bolts and stones, the archers arrows, the spearmen are to launch their missiles … Let stones rain down on the enemy from the allied troops on the higher ground. The combined bombardment from all sides is to be as heavy as possible so as to panic the enemy horses and destroy their riders. It is expected that the indescribable volume of missiles will stop the charging Scythians from coming too close to our infantry line.

(*Ibid.* 25–6)

The Alani were riding into a valley of death. Struck first by the wall of sound from the Roman battle-cry, when they were 500 metres from the Roman battle line they would already be entering a hailstorm of heavy bolts, joined moments later by the lighter bolts of the *manuballistae* and ricocheting stone catapult balls. From 250 metres the stones would be striking them and their horses on first bounce and the storm would be swollen by the archers' war arrows, by the crossfire of sling stones from the flanks, and eventually by hundreds of spears. Arrian confirms that the Alani were unarmoured. If they ever reached the bristling javelin points of the legionary line, with their massed formation riding at, say, 25 km per hour, it would have taken them well over a minute – to use modern timing – to penetrate the 'indescribable volume of missiles'.

40. (Top) The impact of a 70 gram bolt shot from the reconstructed *cheiroballistra* at a range of 50 metres. The target is a replica Roman *lorica segmentata* made of mild steel 1.25 mm thick; the Romans did shoot at their fellow soldiers in several civil wars. The bolt has been reinserted at its angle of strike. It has pierced the outer one of three overlapping plates and dented all of them. It is probable that the shock waves from this sledgehammer blow would have travelled through the stomach and chest cavity and ruptured internal organs, disabling if not killing the soldier. (Photograph © Stuart Williams) (Bottom) Similar damage caused by bolts from the *cheiroballistra* and the three-span Vitruvian *scorpio* at a range of 38 metres. The top plate has been bent inwards into the upper chest area by an 85 gram *cheiroballistra* bolt. (Photograph by the author)

Even during this short time every catapult would have shot at least four missiles, and the two legions' artillery could have launched about six hundred bolts and one hundred bouncing stones. The military philosophy embodied in Arrian's last sentence was to lead ultimately to Emperor Julian's creation of whole legions of artillerymen. The time taken to manufacture six hundred bolts is estimated by Sim and Wilkins as about six hundred hours.

So a full artillery barrage included all these other missiles: stones launched by hand or by sling, javelins and spears by hand or from throwing sticks, and arrows from the composite bows of foot archers or mounted archers.

Vegetius lists the *manuballista* as a catapult operating behind the front line of battle of the *antiqua legio* ('legion of earlier times') and sometimes positioned in the fifth line along with *carroballistae*. He also mentions *manuballistarii* on a siege-tower, joining in with slingers, archers, *arcuballistarii* (using non-torsion crossbows) and others to drive defenders off the walls.

The new design of bolt
The bolts shot by Arrian's *manuballistae* and *carroballistae* were

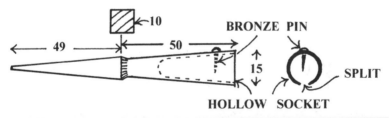

41. One of the bolts suited to the *cheiroballistra* design of catapult, found at Dura Europos in Iraq (see page 33). (Top) Bolt-head of the one complete shaft, redrawn from the excavator's field card in the Yale University archive. (Bottom) The author's replica of the bolt, with oak shaft and flights, and head kindly supplied by John Anstee. The original has an ash shaft and maple flights. The aerodynamic properties and damaging effect of this bolt are discussed on page 54. (Photograph: the author)

very likely of the improved type found at Dura Europos on the Euphrates, and described by Procopius. The open metal framework of these catapults allowed a standard iron bodkin head to be mounted on to a stockier, tapering shaft with wooden flights, too wide to pass through a Vitruvian centre-stanchion (figure 41). One of the advantages of this evil-looking missile over the older dowel-shafted bolts is that its shaft has wounding properties of its own: its expanding profile will create a constantly enlarging entry wound, ripping muscles and crippling, if not killing, men and horses. If it penetrates up to the flights, being of wood these will open the wound further and act like barbs, making removal of the missile extremely difficult and painful. The author's tests found that this bolt is very straight and stable in flight, confirming wind-tunnel tests that have also proved its low ratio of mass to drag; its tail, tapered to fit between the claws of the trigger (figure 31), reduces the turbulence at the rear. One of them caused the damage to the top plate of the *lorica* in figure 40. Our three-span bolts made of straight 18 mm dowelling (figure 20) require very long flights to prevent them rocking in flight.

9
Deciphering the manuscripts: Vitruvius' *ballista*

The Vitruvian stone-thrower, the *ballista*, has been left until last because it is more complex than the bolt-shooter and because there are no archaeological finds of parts. The catapult has to be reconstructed from the text of Vitruvius, the description by Philon of an earlier version of the machine and valuable advice from Heron.

Reliance on Vitruvius' text in the surviving manuscripts is fraught with problems. They are of course all hand copies; the earliest and best one, Harleian 2767 in the British Library, was written *c*.AD 700 by monks in the same writing room as the Lindisfarne Gospels, seven centuries after Vitruvius handed his master copy to his publisher in Rome. Hand-copied manuscripts can be traced back like human family trees; and just as a faulty gene may be inherited, so when a copy of a book is flawed, either because of a copyist's mistake or by physical damage, all copies descending from that one will be liable to repeat the flaw. There are clear signs that Vitruvius' text has suffered badly in transmission. No diagram has survived; Harleian 2767 has blank pages for lost diagrams. Confusions have arisen because Vitruvius wrote both words and cardinal numerals in Roman capital letters. It is easy to forgive the mistakes made by copyists: a typical passage giving the length and width of a part would originally have been written 'LONGITUDOFORAMINISSLATITUDOFORAMINISIS', 'a length of half a hole, a width of one and a half'. Both letter-numerals, S for a half, IS for one and a half, look the same as the end letter(s) of 'FORAMINIS', 'of a hole'. Most Latin manuscripts leave no or very small gaps between words.

Numerals such as VIII or XIIII can easily lose digits. The monks were not engineers and would not have fully understood what they were copying. For fractions, engineers such as Vitruvius used the first letters of the Greek alphabet. Even if the copyist did know the Greek alphabet, he would probably be ignorant of the obsolete digamma **F**, which can be mistaken for a Latin 'F' or 'E', or a Greek gamma. This letter was used by engineers for the numeral 6 and the fraction $^6/_{16}$. The very first numeral in the description of the *ballista* has been corrupted to a word, 'VEL', meaning 'or'. The two strokes of the 'V' may have been miscopied from the numeral II, and the 'E' could originally have been a digamma. The 'L' can be explained as accidental repetition of the first letter of the following word. This is the type of textual detective work

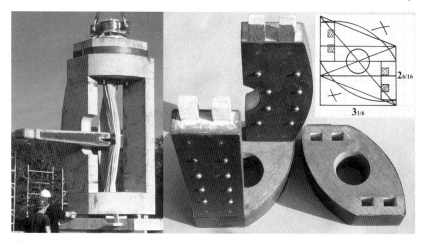

42. Vitruvius' *ballista*. (Left) The $3\frac{1}{2}$ tonne left-hand spring-frame, top washer and arm of the BBC one-talent machine, resting on a cradle of timber that hides the bottom washer. For safety reasons the arm has been braced with iron plates; there is no mention of this in the artillery texts, and the weight of the plates will absorb some of the initial energy in the rope-springs. (Right) The author's scale model of the same spring-frame with the mortise and tenon joints and the iron plating specified by Heron for the sides of the stanchions and hole-carriers. For reasons of expense this plating was omitted on the BBC version. (Top right) Recreation of Vitruvius' missing diagram of the rhombus figure used to draw the outline of the hole-carriers (see page 57). (Photographs: the author)

43. Heron's diagram of the stone-thrower (Wescher's drawing, combining the versions in the Vatican and Paris library copies). In spite of distortions from years of copying and the limitations of incorporating several planes in one drawing, this is a very helpful diagram. It contains two features not in the text: a large horizontal bolt connecting the inner stanchions of the field-frames to the ladder, and the outer crossbars of the yoke system.

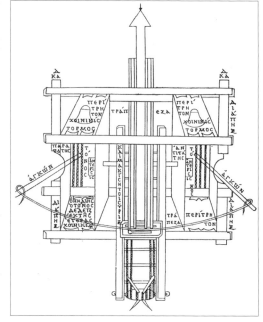

required to produce possible answers to what Vitruvius originally wrote. The resulting measurement, $2^6/16$, makes good sense in the context and unravels the rhombus figure described in the obscure Latin of Vitruvius' opening paragraph. From this rhombus the outline of the hole-carriers can be drawn (figure 42), an elegant geometric solution to the need to increase the strength of the hole-carriers where they have been weakened by the drilling of the spring-hole.

Building the Impossible: the BBC *ballista*

The BBC approached the author for help in constructing the largest possible version of the *ballista*. Throughout Greek and Roman history huge stone-throwers projecting three-talent (78.6 kg) stones seem to have been used only on rare occasions, and usually by a besieging army; few city walls could have accommodated even a half-talent (13 kg) stone-thrower, and very few the one-talent (26.2 kg) machine that we reconstructed. We chose the one-talent size because it appears to be the largest in regular use by the Roman legions, and because the catapult engineer Philon of Byzantium describes it as 'the most violent' stone-thrower and gives detailed instructions for building a triple-ditch system round a city to keep this deadly catapult sufficiently far away to reduce its impact on the walls.

Because Vitruvius was one of four officials appointed by Emperor Augustus to supervise artillery manufacture and repair, his description must represent the official version of the machine in use in the early Roman Empire. The author's revised edition and interpretation of Vitruvius' text formed the basis for our reconstruction of a one-talent machine as used by the Romans at the siege of Jerusalem. Why choose the siege of Jerusalem? Because a graphic eyewitness description of the sight, sound and impact of the one-talent shot is given by the Jewish general Josephus in his *History of the Jewish War*.

The sizes of the components of the catapult were once again calculated in diameters of the rope-spring/spring-hole. Following years of practical experiments the Greek engineers had devised the following formula for calculating this diameter, based on the weight of shot that the catapult was intended to throw: $D = 1.1 \sqrt[3]{(100\,M)}$ where D = the diameter of the spring-hole/rope skein in dactyls and M = the weight of the proposed stone shot in Attic *minae*. The immense precision of the *ballista* design, worked out to cope with the variety of enormous stresses involved, is amply proved by this use of a decimal point and a cube root, the first known appearance of a third degree equation in the history of mathematics.

To project such weights of stone shot a *ballista* had to be capable of withstanding these stresses. Each rope-spring was given a separate, hefty spring-frame of plated timber (figure 42). The pair of frames was

44. Vitruvius' *ballista*. Preparing to slide the stand underneath the one-talent *ballista*, using rollers. Note the two components of the catapult's stock: the long 'ladder' resting on the short 'table'. Also visible are the top and bottom rectangular yoke assemblies that link the two field-frames; they are clearly shown on Heron's diagram in figure 43. The lift is here completed by a modern crane but was started in an authentic Roman way with the two massive 15 metre A-frames and two horizontal all-wood winches each turned by a team of eight. The crane was brought in only when a faulty sheave block collapsed. (Photograph: the author)

clamped in place by substantial top and bottom wooden yoke assemblies. Heron stresses the need to strengthen all critical points with iron plates that must be applied to the sides of the stanchions of the spring-frames, the outside of the hole-carriers and even the tenons of the stanchions inserted into mortises in the hole-carriers.

The case is not made out of a solid beam of timber, which would be impossibly bulky and heavy, but is built as a ladder, with broad side-poles and rungs. This ladder rests on top of the table (figure 44), which in reality is a second ladder with a cover like a table-top. The table braces the ladder and raises it so that its slider holds the stone missile in alignment with the bowstring.

Bowstring problems

Heron (*Belopoiika* 111) says that the stone-thrower's bowstring is not round like the bolt-shooter's, but flat like a belt with a sort of ring in the middle woven from the sinews of which it is constructed. Into this ring fits the single finger of the trigger. The bowstring is positioned so that it catches the middle of the stone missile. 'If it is positioned slightly too high or low it will either travel under the stone or slip over it.' The Kaiser was almost a victim of the *ballista* when Schramm's bowstring slipped under

45. The one-talent Vitruvian *ballista*. The eight-man crew, perhaps numerically the same as its Roman counterpart, is winching the slider forward so that the trigger can be locked on to the bowstring. The 45 degree angle of elevation is too high for shooting to destroy city walls and would be required only for the extreme height of the fortress at Masada (figure 48 and page 63). Our attempt at building a one-talent stone-thrower left us in awe of the complex engineering, which coped with compressional forces measured in hundreds of tons, and it confirmed our respect for the Roman legions' mastery of the supply and construction of huge volumes of timber, metal and sinew-cord. *Ballistarii* were among the specialist soldiers in a legion who were excused fatigues such as guard duty. (Photograph: the author)

the missile, propelling it upwards instead of forwards (figure 8).

Constraints of time meant that we only had three hours to operate the BBC reconstruction – enough for only three shots – and that we did not have time to cope with a second bowstring problem: it stretched so much during the first two shots that the arms smashed into the spring-frames' unplated side-stanchions, causing fatal cracks. Heron (*Belopoiika* 102) emphasises that 'it is necessary to tighten the bowstring sufficiently to hold the arms a short way clear of the side-stanchions, to prevent them being damaged'. The energy remaining after the missile leaves the bowstring is absorbed partly by the bowstring and partly by the arms and the spring-cord as the inner ends of the arms strike Heron's heel-pads, attached to the inner-stanchions.

The stand and the angle of elevation

The design of the stand of the BBC catapult was based on the complex twin-column version introduced by Schramm and Diels. Vitruvius actually lists a single column for the stand, with a width and thickness of $1\frac{1}{2}$ spring-holes as against the $\frac{3}{4}$ of the bolt-shooter's column. There is a good case for believing that Vitruvius' stand was similar to that shown on the Cupid Gem and Trajan's Column, that is a single hefty column braced by two diagonal struts (figure 46).

Vitruvius (*De architectura* X, 11, 9) says that the height of the *ballista*'s stand should be 'as practicality dictates'. Although an elevation of 45 degrees is the theoretical angle for achieving maximum range, field tests with our three-span *scorpio* found that bolts shot at 35 degrees travelled 6–7% further than those from an elevation of 45 degrees. The author's advice to the BBC on attacking a city wall from a 35 degree elevation was not followed (figure 45). The 25 degree elevation of the Cupid Gem case (figure 30) may be close to the authentic angle of elevation for many shooting situations.

46. Vitruvius' *ballista*. The author's scale model, with the curved *regulae* (crossbeams) of the yokes and the special plated wooden washers described in Vitruvius' text. An oval rather than a round hole in the washers allowed extra spring-cord to be inserted to compensate for the space taken up by the washer-bars. Note the design of the stand, based on the text (page 59). The 35 degree angle of elevation is correct for shooting at ramparts and walls, or for launching bouncing shot at enemy personnel. (Photograph: the author)

10
The stone missiles: range and effects

For the effects of the heaviest stone shot there are the more credible parts of the eyewitness description by Josephus, who had been on the receiving end of these missiles at the siege of Jotapata in AD 69: 'more terrifying than the machines themselves was the whizzing sound of the stones' (*History of the Jewish War* III, 247), which 'tore off the battlements and broke off the corners of the towers' (*ibid*. 243). This is reminiscent of First World War descriptions of the sounds of shells passing over. 'There is no body of men strong enough to avoid being flattened right through to the back rank by their force and size' (*ibid*. 244). This is the 'bouncing bomb' effect of stones ricocheting on hard surfaces and causing casualties right to the end of their travel. In contrast, catapult bolts are likely to be effective only on first striking a target. In AD 70 Josephus watched the siege of Jerusalem from the Roman lines, praising the catapults built by the Tenth Legion as superior. 'Their scorpions were more powerful and their stone-throwers larger. The stones which they threw weighed one talent and travelled two stades or more' (*ibid*. 269–70). The distance of two stades (368 metres) is difficult to believe and is usually dismissed as an exaggeration typical of Josephus and/or Roman army propaganda. However, it might be accurate for the

47. Vitruvius' *ballista*. Sculptress Carole Kirsopp cutting by hand a one-talent (26.2 kg) limestone ball. The process begins with mathematical calculations based on the weight of the stone per cubic metre. This gives the required size of cube (left), on to which is scribed a cylinder (centre). The cylinder is then cut into a sphere, one half at a time, a special box (right) being used to support the half-trimmed sphere. The process took two and a half days. (Photographs: the author)

range of the 26 kg shot at the end of its travel after numerous bounces. The rest of Josephus' account sounds authentic:

> Warning of the approach of the stone missiles was given not only by their whizzing sound but also by their whiteness. So sentries were posted on the towers who gave warning whenever the machine was fired and the stone was on the way by shouting in their native tongue 'Sonny's coming'. Those in the path of the missile then scattered and lay flat, the result … was that the stone passed over without causing casualties.
>
> (*ibid.* 271–2)

The Roman answer was to blacken the stones, almost certainly carved from the white limestone of the Mount of Olives; 'they could not be seen so easily and hit their target, killing many with a single shot' (*ibid.* 273).

48. The Tenth Legion's siege of Masada in AD 73. This photograph of the 1966 Masada exhibition shows Eric Marsden's three-span *scorpio* with (top left) some of the bolt-heads found on the site, mounted on modern shafts. The group of stone shot on the left are of grapefruit size; the nearer of the three large stones is *c*.21 kg, the rear two are *c*.26 kg one-talent shot. The huge stone on the right is explained by the excavator Yigael Yadin as a 'rolling stone' prepared by the Jewish defenders to roll down on to the Roman siegeworks. The modern figures in the wall-filling photograph on the right show the enormous scale of the Roman ramp up which the siege-tower was hauled. The possible site for a one-talent *ballista*, suggested by the author on page 63, is marked with an 'x'. (Photograph: Eric Marsden)

So one-talent catapults were lethal against personnel and wooden or lightly built stone battlements but had no significant effect on the walls of Jerusalem, which Herod the Great had rebuilt to the highest specifications with huge blocks of stone.

Masada, AD 73

The Tenth Legion ended the war against the Jews by besieging the final resistance fighters in Herod's spectacular rock fortress of Masada by the Dead Sea. Their giant siege ramp, built upwards from the White Rock, is one of the greatest feats of engineering in the history of siege warfare (figure 48). Yadin's excavations of the rock top uncovered catapult bolt-heads and hundreds of stone missiles. The official report lists stone shot from 0.6 kg to 21 kg in weight but does not record the one-talent (80 Roman *librae*) stones that were found. Two of these were exhibited in the Masada exhibition of 1966 (figure 48). The Masada missiles appear to belong to seven sizes of stone-thrower, of 2, 4, 8, 16, 40, 60 and 80 Roman *librae* calibre. It is possible that, in order to reach the further parts of the rock, 4 *librae* machines were using 2 *librae* ammunition, 16 *librae* shot 8 *librae*, and so on. The fact that one-talent stones have been found on the top demands an explanation. Because of the 1 in 3 slope of the ramp it seems less likely that the Romans followed Demetrius' idea (page 14) and mounted a one-talent catapult in their 27 metre high iron-plated siege-tower. However, if a one-talent machine was positioned at point x in figure 48, at the front end of the White Rock, it could still, in the author's opinion, have hit the casemate wall

49. Yellow-grey sandstone shot from the fortress of Qasr Ibrim on the Nile, dating from *c*.23 BC (page 65). This is BM 71837, one of the seven inscribed *ballista* balls now in The British Museum. It is *c*.16 cm in diameter and weighs 3.9 kg. The top line of the bilingual inscription in black ink is in Greek capital-letter numerals and reads 'ΙΓ' (iota gamma, 10+3 = 13). The bottom line in Roman letters reads 'P' (*ponderis*, 'of weight') XIII. This gives the weight of the shot in Roman *librae* as 13 (4.2 kg). The slight underweight discrepancy is found in one other of the seven missiles and may be explained by drying out of the porous stone. The use of Roman *librae*, rather than the Greek *minae* found on earlier caches of stone shot in the eastern Mediterranean, marks the imposition of the Roman army system in Egypt, which was now under the personal control of Emperor Augustus. The unit involved was perhaps a detachment of the Twenty-Second Legion. (Ten pence piece used as scale. Photograph: the author, by kind permission of the Trustees of The British Museum)

and even cleared it.

A vital piece of evidence on the one-talent's effective range comes from Philon's work *Poliorketika* ('Siege-craft'), dealing specifically with a triple-ditch system to reduce the damage to a city wall by a one-talent machine, 'which is the most violent'. He is talking about an extremely strong defensive wall built of the largest possible blocks of stone. The third of his deep, well-spaced ditches will keep the catapult about 168 metres from the wall so that it 'will strike it with reduced/ weakened force' (Philon, *Poliorketika* 85, 8–10). The 18 metre space between the third and second ditches is to be denied to the catapult by a 'minefield' of thorns, stakes and ditches, the implication being that if the enemy can station the catapult there at about 115 metres from the wall it will seriously damage it. From this it can be argued that although at a range of 168 metres the stone was losing the power to do serious damage to a strong wall of large stones, it had by no means reached its maximum, first bounce range, which might be near the 200 metre mark. This is the only hard evidence for the performance of the Hellenistic stone-thrower; but Vitruvius' washer design and larger spring-frames allowed more spring-cord to be inserted. So a Vitruvian one-talent catapult positioned at the front of the White Rock and elevated at about 50 degrees could probably have reached the Jews' battlements and

50. Burnswark native hillfort, Dumfriesshire, and the southern of the two Roman camps. This aerial photograph of May 1980, one of the last taken by Professor Kenneth St Joseph, shows the prominent rampart and ditches of the southern camp, with the three mounds outside the camp entrances at the foot of the hill. Professor George Jobey's excavations showed that the hillfort's defences (faintly visible in this photograph) were already in ruins when they became the target of Roman slingshot, archers' triple-barbed arrows and stone missiles. Therefore the site was probably a Roman training school for practising siege warfare, and the mounds are to be interpreted as artillery platforms for archers, slingers and stones shot from catapults or thrown by hand or with throwing sticks. The use of the camp for this purpose may date from the Antonine period or as late as the early third century (see page 78). (Photograph © Cambridge University Collection of Air Photographs)

51. (Left) Lead sling bullet of lemon shape from Burnswark, found east of the hill close to Burnswark Farm on the right edge of figure 50. Undamaged and possibly never used; weight 50 grams, length 2.8 cm. About 140 lead bullets have been recorded from the site, most of them clustered around the three entrances of the hillfort. (Photograph: the author) (Centre) Accurately dressed sandstone artillery ball in Dumfries Museum, from the slope below Shan Castle Iron Age hillfort, Dumfriesshire. Weighs 2.25 Roman *librae* (0.74 kg), diameter 8 cm. This is similar in size and finish to several of the sandstone balls from Burnswark and is suitable for a 2 *librae ballista*, the smallest stone-thrower in Vitruvius' list (page 15). It does not sit comfortably in the hand and is unlikely to have been intended for throwing either by hand or by means of a *fustibalus* (arm-extending stick with a sling). The smaller stones of about 0.17 and 0.34 kg from Burnswark were most likely thrown by hand, or with the arm extension afforded by the *fustibalus*. (Photograph: the author, by kind permission of Dumfries and Galloway Museums) (Right) Roman auxiliaries preparing to throw stones by hand and by sling, Trajan's Column, Scene LXVI. (Cast in the Museo della Civiltà Romana, EUR, Rome. Photograph: the author)

perhaps beyond. If it failed to do so, the answer would have been to use a one-and-a-half-talent machine to fire one-talent stones.

Qasr Ibrim: inscribed stone shot

Some of the important inscribed stones from the fortified site of Qasr Ibrim, towering above the Nile near Abu Simbel, have weights of 3, 9 and 13 *librae* marked in Greek and Latin (figure 49); the weights of others match calibres 15, 17, 19, 21 and 23 *librae*. The height of the battlements above the Nile would have added to the range and impact of these missiles and probably accounts for the lack of larger calibres.

Stone-throwers on the northern frontier

Archaeological evidence attests the presence of stone-throwers of up to one- and one-and-a-half-talent sizes on the northern frontier of Britain during the period from Hadrian to the reign of Severus Alexander, AD 225–35. The sites are the Hadrianic fort at Halton Chesters, the outpost forts at Risingham and High Rochester, and the Roman camps and artillery mounds at Burnswark. See figures 50, 51 and 56, and page 79.

11
The one-arm and Hatra stone-throwers

The 'one-arm' stone-thrower

The most elusive Graeco-Roman catapult is the Greek *monangkon* ('one-arm'), known in later Roman times as the *onager* ('wild ass'). It is first mentioned by Philon in a passage on defending a city under siege: 'You must try to smash through the roofs of the siege-sheds by releasing very large stones from machines and projecting beams, and by shooting from above with one-talent and one-arm stone-throwers' (Philon, *Poliorketika* 91, 33–8). This defines the one-arm as a heavy stone-thrower on a par with the very powerful one-talent *ballista*. Nothing more is heard of it until the early second century AD when Trajan's engineer Apollodorus describes a one-arm mounted on the front of a battering ram that is suspended from siege-ladders (figure 52). 'The ram is thrust forward from the ladders, and when it is brought to bear on the wall it will release and fire the one-arm at the defenders, resulting in the defeat of those who stand in its path' (Apollodorus, *Poliorketika* 188). Again the implication is that the one-arm is capable of releasing an extremely heavy stone.

This is confirmed by Ammianus Marcellinus, the fourth-century historian and army officer, who operated these stone-throwers in Emperor Julian's campaign against the Persians (AD 363). He gives a general description of the machine, with its single vertical wooden pole (arm) inserted into the single rope skein and striking a huge buffer padded with fine chaff. A sling of iron or flax hangs from hooks on the top of the arm.

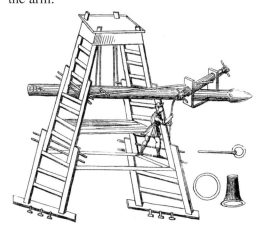

52. Manuscript diagram of a one-arm stone-thrower mounted on a battering ram suspended from a large ladder-tower (see above). Note the three-section ladder construction locked together by long pins, an indication of the structure's portability. Such a ladder-tower could be rapidly set up for mounting an artillery piece in a situation such as that at Hod Hill (page 21). (After Wescher 1867)

When the battle begins, a round stone is placed in the sling and four young men on each side wind back the bars ... and pull the pole down almost horizontal. Finally the master artilleryman, standing by and rising to his full height, disengages the pin ... with a sledgehammer; ... the pole is released ... and when it contacts the soft hair cloth it hurls the stone, which will smash whatever it hits.

(Ammianus, *History* XXIII, 6)

Unfortunately Ammianus does not describe the upper framework that holds the huge buffer. There are two modern solutions to this, the first being the 'railway buffer' design, tested by Sir Ralph Payne-Gallwey in the early twentieth century. His 2 ton *onager* without a sling hurled a 3.64 kg stone from 320 to 330 metres, but when fitted with a sling the range increased to 412 to 420 metres, and at full tension to nearly 457 metres. The second possible design was built by Schramm and improved by Marsden (figure 53). Schramm's large *onager* and Marsden's small one reached over 300 metres with unspecified missiles.

53. The one-arm *onager*. (Top left) Version built for the Ermine Street Guard by Len Morgan, based on the reconstruction by Sir Ralph Payne-Gallwey. (Photograph: The Ermine Street Guard) (Top right) Schramm's *onager*. There is no evidence that wheels were fitted directly to any Roman catapult. (After Schramm 1918/1980) (Bottom left) Model by the author. (Photograph: the author) (Bottom right) Version by Eric Marsden. (Photograph: Eric Marsden)

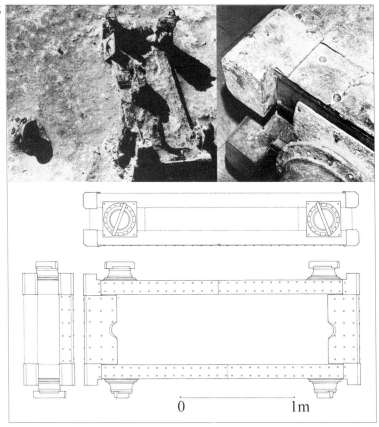

54. The Hatra stone-thrower. (Top left) The frame and its washers as excavated. It has fallen face down with the case and slider pointing up in the air. Case, slider and all but a few fragments of the wood frame have rotted away, leaving the 2 mm thick bronze sheets that clad the frame, and the bronze washers with their underplates and badly corroded iron washer-bars. One washer has rolled away to the side of the photograph. The stump of the end of the case or its bracket is visible in the middle of the bottom frame. (Photograph: W. I. Al-Salihi, Directorate-General of Antiquities, Baghdad) (Top right) Detail of the elegant cast-bronze fittings covering the corner joints of the wood frame, as restored in the Mosul Museum, Baghdad. (Photograph: Dietwulf Baatz) (Bottom) Schematic drawing of the parts of the metal frame, from above, the side and the front. (Dietwulf Baatz)

The enormous power of Ammianus' machine is confirmed by the fact that it took eight men to wind back the arm, and a sledgehammer blow to overcome the friction on the trigger. It is quite possible that a very large *onager* could project even heavier stones than a three-talent two-arm stone-thrower. Lurid proof of the *onager*'s power is Ammianus' account of the engineer standing behind one, who was killed when an artilleryman was careless in loading the stone in the sling and it shot backwards, destroying the engineer so disastrously that not all the pieces of his body could be identified (*ibid.* XXIV, 4). Ammianus mentions the special resilient platforms of turf or thin bricks needed to cope with the machine's violent recoil (it is the only catapult with recoil); he also emphasises its lack of mobility in his description of the difficulties of moving four *onagri* overnight to a new defensive position; the effort was worthwhile because the *onagri* smashed the iron-clad Persian siege-towers (*ibid.* XIX, 7).

In spite of the dearth of references to this catapult in surviving sources, it may well have been used not infrequently in sieges from the Hellenistic period onwards, until it became the only stone-thrower used in the later Roman Empire. It was much simpler to make, adjust and operate than the two-arm machines; it only had one spring and so did not use as much sinew-rope. It could probably cope with heavier missiles and, by adjusting the length of its sling and so its trajectory, it could be made to lob missiles over high obstacles or bowl them along the ground against personnel. It may be that the two-arm stone-thrower's complexity was the cause of its decline. When it disappeared from use is unknown.

The Hatra stone-thrower

Part of the spring-frame of an unfamiliar design of stone-thrower dating from the third century AD was found at Hatra in Iraq in 1972. Hatra's superb defensive walls and artillery had driven Trajan's army away in AD 117; and when Severus assaulted the city in 198 his men suffered very heavy casualties and his machines were burned by artillery fire. His second assault failed; the historian Dio records that 'he lost ... all his catapults, except those constructed by Priscus, and many troops' (Dio Cassius, *Roman History* LXXVI, 11). The Hatra artillery was so effective at long range that 'they even hit many of Severus' bodyguards, shooting two missiles simultaneously from the same discharge' (*ibid.*). When Roman troops approached the wall and began to breach it, the Hatreni 'amongst other things shot bituminous naphtha at them which burned the artillery and all the soldiers struck by it' (*ibid.*). The naphtha was probably delivered by the special artillery bolts with 'cage' points (figure 22), one of which took Dr David Sim nearly three hours to recreate.

The 1972 catapult find belongs to the last phase of the city's life, when it was suffering attacks from the Sassanids. The Hatreni appear to have asked for Roman help because two inscriptions record the presence of a Roman cohort, *cohors IX Mauretanorum*, under Gordian III (AD 238–44). The catapult may have been one of the Hatreni's own but is equally likely to have been a Roman army one; if the latter, it attests the operation of catapults by an auxiliary unit. Two of its features are also characteristic of the *cheiroballistra*: its springs are mounted far apart in

55. The Hatra stone-thrower. (Top) The author's interpretation of the Hatra spring-frame, with the stanchions marked in black. By turning the stanchion design of the Vitruvian *ballista* (figure 23) through 90 degrees, frame intrusion on arm travel is markedly reduced, allowing the bowstring to travel further forward before hitting the rear stanchion. The two spring-frames are 2.25 times further apart than the Vitruvian ones, postponing the moment when the critical

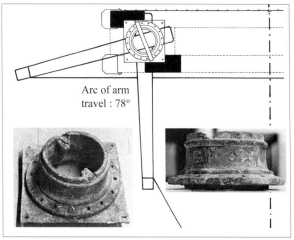

Arc of arm travel : 78°

150 degree final bowstring-to-arm angle is reached and so enabling the arms to be pulled further to the rear (see page 42). The total gain is a vital extra 13 degrees of arm travel, and, as for the *cheiroballistra*, an improved view of the target and so more accurate aiming. (Bottom) One of the bronze washers, superbly designed and cast, with a reinforcing ring below the top, and inner lugs supporting the iron washer-bars against the compressive force of the spring-cord. Each washer has a square underplate protecting the wooden frame against wear. The 16 cm spring diameter is similar to that of a Vitruvian 5 *librae ballista*, but the volume of the spring-cord will have been less because the ratio of spring diameter to spring height is only 1:6.65, as against the Vitruvian 1:9.4. The increased arc of the Hatra arm travel may have made up all, or nearly all, of the difference. (Photographs: Dietwulf Baatz)

a very wide frame, and the frames are squatter and the spring volume less than that of a Vitruvian *ballista* with the same spring diameter. These two facts lend support to the theory that this stone-thrower is the Roman army's redesign of the Vitruvian *ballista*, a parallel exercise to their work on the *cheiroballistra*. The Hatra frame is still made of wood, faced with 2 mm thick bronze sheets, possibly because even the heaviest manageable metal spring-frame would not have been able to cope with the enormous compressive and torsional stresses of a stone-thrower. Little more than the front of the spring-frame's plating survives, together with its superb bronze washers (figure 54), the catapult having fallen from Tower 19 and landed face downwards with its case and slider vertical. The latter and the back of the spring-frame have rotted away. The modern theory that this catapult had inward-swinging arms would require the spring-frame to be moved from the front to the middle of the case; this is disproved by the way it has landed. The author believes that the unusual position of the semicircular cut-outs in the front plates (figure 54) is evidence that the engineers had found a new answer to the problem of allowing a wider arc for the arms without weakening the spring-frame (figure 55).

12
Survival

The one-arm *onager* is the only type of stone-thrower known to Vegetius, the late-fourth-century writer on the Roman army. It was perhaps the only torsion-powered stone-thrower to survive until medieval times, if indeed it is the same as the *mangonel*.

However, torsion bolt-shooters of the *cheiroballistra* type continued in use. There is a fifth-century inscription from Cherson (Crimea) mentioning *ballistarii*, *ballista* mechanics or artillerymen. *Polemikai hamaxai meta cheirotoxobolistron* ('war wagons with hand-arrow-shooters' – note the last word's close resemblance to *cheiroballistra*) were used by the people of Cherson in the late third and fourth centuries. *Carroballistae* are mentioned in tactical manuals of the seventh (Maurice's *Strategicon*) and tenth centuries (Leo's *Tactica*).

The powerful psychological effect of the bolt-shooter's accuracy continued to be attested. Procopius records an incident in the siege of Rome by the Goths in AD 536 when a tower-mounted catapult shot a bolt that passed through the breastplate and body of a distinguished Gothic warrior and sank to over half its length in a tree. The sight of the warrior's corpse pinned to the tree caused utter panic amongst the Goths and they stayed out of missile range. The Byzantine historian John Scylitzes describes how a bolt-shooter defending a Byzantine camp *c.*AD 1050 saved the day when the leader of a tribe besieging the camp was run through and impaled on his horse *katapeltiko belei* ('with a bolt from a catapult').

On this evidence it appears that torsion artillery, invented *c.*350 BC, was still used by Byzantine armies *c.*AD 1050, giving it a remarkable life span of fourteen centuries. The *cheiroballistra* type of bolt-shooter, in use by *c.*AD 100, seems to have lasted more than nine centuries.

56. One of the two inscriptions from the fort at High Rochester, Northumberland, recording the construction of *ballistaria*, emplacements for artillery, by the First Loyal Cohort of the Vardulli, a one-thousand-strong, part-mounted infantry unit. This one, R.I.B. 1280, dates from AD 220, the second, R.I.B. 1281, from 225–35 (after Richmond). The design of the *ballistaria* is unknown. Were they simply bases to raise catapults to a shooting position, or did they

incorporate frontal protection and/or overhead covers? They may have been intended for two-arm stone-throwers of Vitruvian (or Hatran) type, as attested by the one-talent and one-and-a-half-talent shot found at this site (page 79) and at the fort of Risingham. Were auxiliary units such as the Vardulli allowed by this date to operate artillery without legionary help?

13
The Roman achievement

It has been claimed that the Romans made few improvements to the Greek artillery designs that they adopted. That this is untrue of the period of the Roman Empire has been demonstrated above, firstly in the case of Vitruvius' *ballista*, whose reshaped spring-frames and special washers increased the power of the machine. Secondly, a case has been made for the Hatra stone-thrower being the Roman army's replacement of the Vitruvian machine with a completely new spring-frame design permitting increased arm travel and power.

Thirdly, Marsden was right to list the *cheiroballistra* as a new category of bolt-shooter rather than as the Mark VI version of the Hellenistic machine, because the *cheiroballistra* and its larger brothers do not simply represent a replacement of wood by metal, but a new design of frame, arms and stand. The 'safety' of the well-tried Hellenistic plated-wood version was abandoned and the challenge undertaken to create entirely in metal a frame whose characteristics produced increased power. The greater stresses to which the new material would be subjected would have been unpredictable and potentially dangerous. A bold, thorough programme of strain testing during the development stage is implied.

A second charge levelled against the Romans is that they never attained the mechanical standards of the Greeks. The author of the *Cheiroballistra* text is Greek, and the expertise of Greek artillery engineers, like that of Greek doctors, continued to be consulted. However, the new frame, arms and stand must surely have evolved from the legions' own thorough reappraisal of user requirements and desired weapon characteristics. The success of this family of bolt-shooters must be credited to them and to the superb quality of Roman metalwork produced by the legionary *fabricae* and by the specialist smiths of Autun (central France), Trier (west Germany) and other centres appointed by the high command to manufacture *ballistae*. Their success also exposes the folly of Frontinus' pessimistic view (*Stratagems* III, preface), expressed around the time when the new catapults were at the design or even trials stage, that the development of engines of war had long ago reached its limit.

In 399 BC engineers working for Dionysius of Syracuse had initiated the development of Greek artillery by greatly increasing the size and power of the composite Scythian bow beyond that of the hand-drawn weapon. This approach was paralleled by the Chinese development of gigantic multiple bows capable of extreme ranges but with the sacrifice of mobility and speed of operation. At the end of a long line of development of torsion artillery the compact and portable *cheiroballistra* and its larger brothers represent one of the most impressive and efficient designs of bolt-shooters in the history of warfare.

14
Sources and references to artillery

Ancient sources

Philon of Byzantium

Possibly active in the last half of the third century BC. He cites his long association with the Alexandrian artillery technicians and his contacts with many master craftsmen of Rhodes. His works include *Paraskeuastika* ('Siege Preparations') and *Poliorketika* ('Siege-craft'). His *Belopoiika* ('Artillery Construction'), translated by Marsden, contains measurements for parts of the Hellenistic stone-thrower which can often be used to supply or correct missing or corrupt measurements in Vitruvius' *ballista* text. Unfortunately his diagrams, like those of Vitruvius, have not survived.

Vitruvius

His *De architectura* ('On engineering and architecture'), published *c.*25 BC, is the only surviving work on the subject and has had a profound influence on western architecture. He was a catapult specialist and, along with three others, was put in charge of the construction and repair of artillery by Augustus, having also served Julius Caesar, probably in the same capacity. Therefore his description of the bolt-shooting *scorpio* and stone-throwing *ballista* must represent the standard versions used by the early imperial army. His diagrams have not survived. The version of his *ballista* text published by Schramm often strays some way from the manuscript evidence, and the present author has revised the text for both machines (available on the author's website).

Heron of Alexandria

One of the great Alexandrian engineers. He witnessed the eclipse of the moon in AD 62 and is assumed to have worked in the second half of the first century AD, possibly surviving into the second century. His *Belopoiika* ('Artillery Construction'), translated by Marsden, contains a review of the development of artillery from stomach-bow to torsion weapons, and much catapult lore on building and setting up the catapults, with particular emphasis on the stone-thrower. His diagrams do survive, but he does not give measurements for parts (unless he put this information in a section that has not survived). The *Cheiroballistra* text is not in his style and is unlikely to have been written by him.

Josephus

His eyewitness account of the Roman war against the Jews (AD 66–73) is translated with parallel Greek text by H. St J. Thackeray in volumes 2 and 3 of the Loeb Classical Library edition of Josephus (Heinemann and Harvard, 1927). The 1959 translation by G. A. Williamson, *Josephus: The Jewish War*, is published in the Penguin Classics series. Williamson translates the word for scorpions as 'quick-firers'.

Arrian

General and historian. Appointed by Hadrian as governor of Cappadocia (east Turkey), he defeated the invasion by the hordes of Alani in AD 134. His order of march and briefing for the battle with the Alani survive (page 51).

Vegetius
His *Epitoma rei militaris* is the only manual on the Roman army to have survived intact. It was written sometime after AD 383 but is a scissors and paste assembly of material from various periods in the history of the army. There is an English translation by N. P. Milner, *Vegetius, Epitome of Military Science* (Liverpool University Press, 1993).

Accounts of Roman artillery in action
The scope of this book does not allow the inclusion of the many accounts of artillery in action from the works of ancient authors. For these the reader should consult the relevant sections of Marsden's first volume, *Historical Development*, particularly Section III, 'The spread of artillery in the west', Section V, 'Artillery in sieges', Section VII, 'Catapults in field campaigns and naval warfare', and Section VIII, 'Roman imperial artillery', important for the raising of whole legions of *ballistarii* in the fourth century. Marsden does not often translate his Latin and Greek quotations. Most sources are translated in the Loeb Classical Library series, many in the Penguin Classics series.

Select bibliography
Most of the important articles are scattered in specialist journals, but they can be found in certain major British libraries and some university collections. Most of the volumes of the *Journal of Roman Military Equipment Studies*, abbreviated below as *JRMES*, are available from Oxbow Press, Park End Place, Oxford OX1 1HN.

Baatz, D. 'Recent finds of ancient artillery', *Britannia*, 9 (1978), 1–17. Important for the publication of the Hatra, Gornea and Orşova finds.

Baatz, D. 'Ein katapult der Legio IV Macedonica aus Cremona', *Römische Mitteilungen*, 87 (1980), 283–99. The full publication of the Cremona shield, washers, and other finds.

Baatz, D. *Bauten und Katapulte des römischen Heeres*. Franz Steiner Verlag, Stuttgart, 1994. This volume reprints all of Baatz's artillery articles and adds new chapters.

Baatz, D., and Feugère, M. 'Éléments d'une catapulte Romaine trouvée à Lyon', *Gallia*, 39 (1981), 201–9. The Lyon spring-frame and washers.

Birley, A. *Garrison Life at Vindolanda*. Tempus, 2002. See pages 114–16 for the account mentioning sinew.

Bishop, M. C., and Coulston, J. C. N. *Roman Military Equipment*. Batsford, 1993. Includes many illustrations and references to artillery.

Campbell, D. B. 'Ballistaria in first to mid-third century Britain', *Britannia*, 15 (1984), 75–84. Important discussion on the claimed identification of artillery emplacements in forts at Hod Hill, High Rochester and others.

Campbell, D. B. 'Auxiliary artillery revisited', *Bonner Jahrbücher*, 186 (1986), 117–32. Was artillery ever used by non-legionary troops? Valuable discussions on Hatra and High Rochester, among others.

Connolly, P. *Greece and Rome at War*. Macdonald, 1981. Valuable sections are shared with Dr Roger Tomlin on the later Roman army and siege warfare.

Gudea, N., and Baatz, D. 'Teile spätrömischer ballisten aus Gornea und Orşova', *Saalburg Jahrbuch*, 31 (1974), 50–72. Gives the full details of the Gornea and Orşova finds.

Hart, V. G., and Lewis, M. J. T. 'Mechanics of the *onager*', *Journal of Engineering and Mathematics*, 20 (1986), 345–65.

Hassall, M. 'Perspectives on Greek and Roman catapults', *Archaeology International* (1999), 23–6.

James, S. T. 'Archaeological evidence for Roman incendiary projectiles', *Saalburg Jahrbuch*, 39 (1983), 142–3.

James, S. T., and Taylor, J. H. 'Parts of artillery projectiles from Qasr Ibrim, Egypt', *Saalburg Jahrbuch*, 47 (1997), 93–8.

Jobey, G. 'Burnswark Hill', *Transactions of the Dumfriesshire and Galloway Natural History and Antiquarian Society*, 53 (1977–8), 57–104. Includes excavations on the Roman camps and a summary of the missile finds.

Landels, J. G. *Engineering in the Ancient World*. Chatto & Windus, 1978. Chapter 5 (pages 99–132) discusses the engineering principles of ancient artillery.

Lepper, F., and Frere, S. S. *Trajan's Column*. Alan Sutton, 1988. See pages 105–7 for the artillery scenes.

Marsden, E. W. *Greek and Roman Artillery: Historical Development*. Oxford, 1969. Reprinted by Sandpiper, 1999. An indispensable, masterly survey of the historical background and defensive systems.

Marsden, E. W. *Greek and Roman Artillery: Technical Treatises*. Oxford, 1971. Reprinted by Sandpiper, 1999. Excellent editions, with English translations and discussion, of the Greek texts of Heron and Philon. Marsden's early death prevented his intended revision of the sections on Vitruvius and the *cheiroballistra*.

Maxwell, G. *A Gathering of Eagles: Scenes from Roman Scotland*. Historic Scotland, 1998. An important reassessment of the camps at Burnswark.

Payne-Gallwey, R. *The Crossbow (with ... an Appendix on the Catapult, Balista and Turkish Bow)*. London, 1907.

Richmond, I. A. *Hod Hill Volume II: Excavations Carried Out between 1951 and 1958*. London, 1968. See pages 32–3 and figure 14 for the artillery barrage.

Schramm, Erwin. *Die antiken Geschütze der Saalburg*. 1918. Reprinted with an introduction by D. Baatz, Saalburg Museum, 1980. An indispensable classic from one of the great exponents of experimental archaeology.

Sim, D., and Ridge, I. *Iron for the Eagles: The Iron Industry of Roman Britain*. Tempus, 2002. Includes Sim's authoritative experiments on the manufacture of weapons.

Stevenson, D. 'The manufacture of sinew rope', *Journal of the Society of Archer-Antiquaries*, 40 (1997), 13–17. The first successful recreation of catapult sinew-rope in modern times.

Todd, M. *The Walls of Rome*. Paul Elek, 1978. Includes an 87 BC catapult emplacement in figure 4, and other references to artillery on the later walls.

Wilkins, A. 'Reconstructing the *cheiroballistra*', *JRMES*, 6 (1995), 5–59. Includes text, translation and reconstruction as a winched bolt-shooter.

Wilkins, A. '*Scorpio* and *cheiroballistra*', *JRMES*, 11 (2000), 77–101. The *scorpio* is reconstructed from revised text and finds of parts. Also includes an update on the *cheiroballistra*.

Wilkins, A. 'The Graeco-Roman stone-throwing catapult', *Timber Framing*, 65 (September 2002), 18–19. With articles on building and lifting the BBC *ballista* by Gordon Macdonald and Professor Grigg Mullen Jr.

Websites

There are many websites offering information on Greek and Roman artillery, much of which is erroneous. The best site, with scholarly information and references, is that maintained by Professor Dr Dietwulf Baatz, *Catapults in Greek and Roman Antiquity* (http://home.t-online.de/home/d.baatz/catapult.htm).

There is an illustrated section on artillery on the website of the Roman Military Research Society (www.romanarmy.net).

The author is building up his own site (www.alanwilkins.org). It will provide access to a revised text of Vitruvius' *scorpio* and *ballista*, and updated versions of articles on these catapults, Dionysius' repeating bolt-shooter, and the *cheiroballistra*. Translations will be available of works on siege-craft by Philon and others.

Television programmes

Some television programmes deal specifically with the subject and are regularly repeated.

What the Romans Did for Us. Part Two: *Invasion*. BBC2, 2000. (Produced by Martin Mortimore.) Adam Hart-Davis examines the role of artillery. The Roman Military Research Society demonstrates the *scorpio, onager* and *manuballista*. Len Morgan shoots the *scorpio* on Hod Hill, and the author demonstrates his reconstruction of Dionysius' repeating catapult complete with the double-chain drive.

Building the Impossible. The Roman War Machine. BBC2, 2002. (Produced by Helen Thomas.) The construction of the one-talent stone-thrower.

Ancient Discoveries. Part Three: *Heron of Alexandria*. Discovery Channel, 2003. (Produced by Stuart Clarke.) A tribute to Heron and the engineers of Alexandria; includes Dionysius' repeating bolt-shooter and the *cheiroballistra*.

15
Museums and sites

Museums

Many museums in the area of the Roman Empire display artillery bolt-heads. The following list selects only those museums with important artillery finds or reconstructions on display.

BRITAIN

Chesterholm Museum, Vindolanda, Bardon Mill, Hexham, Northumberland NE47 7JN. Telephone: 01434 344277. Website: www.vindolanda.com Has an exceptional variety of missile heads, and a replica of the 'sinew' document (page 36).

Dewa Roman Experience, Pierpoint Lane, Off Bridge Street, Chester, Cheshire CH1 1NL. Telephone: 01244 343407. Website: www.cheshire.gov.uk/tourism Has a small working model *onager*.

Dorset County Museum, High West Street, Dorchester, Dorset DT1 1XA. Telephone: 01305 262735. Website: www.dorsetcountymuseum.org Includes an exhibit of the Maiden Castle victims (figure 6). The square hole in one skull was most likely caused by a Roman arrow rather than a catapult bolt.

Dumfries Museum, The Observatory, Dumfries, Dumfries and Galloway DG2 7SW. Telephone: 01387 253374. Website: www.dumgal.gov.uk/museums Displays Burnswark and Shan Castle stone shot, and Burnswark sling bullets (figure 51).

Hunterian Museum, Gilbert-Scott Building, University Avenue, The University of Glasgow, Glasgow G12 8QQ. Telephone: 0141 330 4221. Website: www.hunterian.gla.ac.uk Stone shot and composite bow nocks from Bar Hill Roman fort are exhibited.

Museum of Antiquities, The University of Newcastle upon Tyne, Newcastle upon Tyne NE1 7RU. Telephone: 0191 222 7849. Website: www.ncl.ac.uk/antiquities Houses High Rochester *ballistaria* inscriptions (figure 56), large stone shot and bolt-heads.

National Museums of Scotland, Chambers Street, Edinburgh EH1 1JF. Telephone: 0131 225 7534. Website: www.nms.ac.uk Stone shot and sling bullets from Burnswark are on display.

Roman Baths Museum, Pump Room, Stall Street, Bath, Somerset BA1 1LZ. Telephone: 01225 477773. Website: www.romanbaths.co.uk Exhibits a small bronze washer, spring diameter 34 mm, possibly from a small training model catapult (figure 11). Thrown as an offering into the sacred spring, perhaps by an engineer hoping for Sulis Minerva's help.

Royal Armouries at Fort Nelson, Fort Nelson, Fareham, Hampshire PO17 6AN. Telephone: 01329 233734. Website: www.armouries.org.uk Houses Sir Ralph Payne-Gallwey's large *onager* (page 67).

Tullie House Museum and Art Gallery, Castle Street, Carlisle, Cumbria CA3 8TP. Telephone: 01228 534781. Website: www.tulliehouse.co.uk A *cheiroballistra* reconstruction and a small working model *onager* are on display, as well as bolt-heads, stone shot and Burnswark sling bullets.

FRANCE

Musée de la Civilisation Gallo-Romaine, 17, Rue de Cleberg, Lyon. Houses the Lyon field-frame (figure 47).

Musée des Antiquités Nationales, Chateau – Place Charles de Gaulle, 78100 St-Germain-en-Laye. Telephone: 0033 (0)1 39 10 13 00. Website: www.museeantiquitesnationales.fr Victor Prou's reconstruction of the *cheiroballistra* is on display.

GERMANY
Limesmuseum, St Johann Strasse 5, 73430 Aalen, Baden-Wurttemberg. Has a replica of the Caminreal frame.
Saalburgmuseum, Saalburg-Kastell, 61350 Bad Homburg vor der Höhe. Telephone: 0049 (0)6175 93740. Website: www.saalburgmuseum.de Those of Schramm's catapults that survived the Second World War are on display in the museum of the reconstructed fort.

ITALY
Museo Civico, Palazzo Affaitati, via Ugulani Dati 4, Cremona. The Cremona shield is on display.
Museo della Civiltà Romana, Piazza G. Agnelli, 00144 Roma. This is at EUR, near the station EUR Fermi on Linea B of the Rome Metro. The casts of Trajan's Column are at eye-level but are broken up into short lengths.
Musei Vaticani, Viale Vaticano-00165, Città del Vaticano, Roma. The Vedennius tombstone (figure 13) is in the Chiaramonti Gallery (a statue of Diana stands on top of it). Trajan's Column is in the Roman Forum. A pair of binoculars and/or a 35 mm camera with a 30 or 40 cm telephoto lens are essential to pick out the artillery scenes on it.

SPAIN
Museo Arqueológico de Catalunya-Empúries, 17130 Empúries-L'Escala, Catalunya. A replica of the Ampurias frame (figure 9) is on display.
Museo Provincial de Teruel, Plaza Fray Anselmo Polanco, Apartado de Correos 119, 44071 Teruel, Aragon. Exhibits the Caminreal catapult frame (figure 10), and washers from Azaila.
Museu Arqueològic Barcelona, Pg. de Santa Madrona 39–41, Barcelona 08038. Houses the Ampurias catapult frame.

Sites
There are very few sites in Britain where artillery is known to have been in action because there are no accounts of long sieges of impregnable strongholds such as Jerusalem and Masada.

Sites from the Roman invasion
Hod Hill, Dorset (page 21). Ordnance Survey sheet 194, NGR 8510. Access is from the village of Stourpaine. The site of the 'chieftain's hut' is not marked, but its approximate position can be worked out from Richmond's article.
Maiden Castle, Dorset (page 20). Ordnance Survey sheet 194, NGR 6788, 2 km south-west of Dorchester, off the A354. It is worth visiting the Dorset County Museum in Dorchester first to see the victims of what was probably only a brief assault.

The northern frontier
Burnswark Roman Camps, Dumfries and Galloway (see figure 50). Ordnance Survey sheet 85, NGR 1878. Access is by the unclassified road that leaves the B725 by the railway bridge 1 km north-east of Ecclefechan. After 3 km on this unclassified road, park at the T-junction (near the bottom left corner of figure 50). The two Roman camps may have been first constructed during the military advance by governor Petillius Cerialis *c*.AD 72–3. Gordon Maxwell's *A Gathering of Eagles* should be read before visiting the site.

High Rochester Roman fort, Northumberland. Ordnance Survey sheet 80, NGR 8398. Before exploring the impressive remains of this outpost fort of Hadrian's Wall, it is worth visiting the Museum of Antiquities at the University of Newcastle upon Tyne to see the two third-century inscriptions from the site mentioning the repair of *ballistaria*, emplacements for catapults (figure 56). The three large stone catapult balls on display in the museum weigh 24, 28 and 42 kg, the first two being suitable for a one-talent (80 *librae*) stone-thrower, and the 42 kg shot implying the presence at High Rochester of a one-and-a-half-talent machine.

Later Roman coastal defences

Burgh Castle, Norfolk. Ordnance Survey sheet 134, NGR 4704. Signposted from the roundabout on the A149, 3 km north of Great Yarmouth. The impressive remains of one of the Saxon Shore forts that protected the coast against Saxon raids in the late third century AD. The huge drum of the fallen bastion of the south wall has a round socket that may be part of a revolving base for a catapult, possibly a large bolt-shooter of the type and size of the Orşova arch (page 48). All these coastal forts would have been well equipped with both bolt- and stone-shooting catapults.

Index

Page numbers in italic refer to illustrations